THE ESSENTIAL
LITTLE CRUISE BOOK

"Cruisers will find noteworthy nuggets in *The Essential Little Cruise Book* by veteran cruise director Jim West."

—*New York Post*

"Nuggets of wisdom from a veteran cruise director ... a real charmer."

—*Chicago Tribune*

"A pocket-sized treasure-trove of tips for both first-time cruisers and old salts."

—Charles Doherty, managing editor, *Cruise Travel Magazine*

"A store of helpful hints to make your journey aboard a cruise ship smooth sailing all the way."

—*Navy Times*

"*The Essential Little Cruise Book* is the next best thing to having your travel agent cruise with you.... Don't leave home without it."

—Debbie Natansohn,
executive vice president, Orient Lines

"Cruise veteran Jim West knows the Seven Seas as he knows what makes a cruise safe, economical, and enjoyable. His book is packed with tips for travelers—hundreds of ways to enjoy cruising without glitches or gaffes. The sections on choosing a travel agent and a cruise line, how and what to pack, and how to survive on five meals a day—these alone are worth the cost of this fun book."

—Voit Gilmore, former president,
American Society of Travel Agents

THE ESSENTIAL LITTLE CRUISE BOOK

Secrets from a
Cruise Director for a Perfect
Cruise Vacation

Second Edition

Jim West

The Globe Pequot Press

Guilford, Connecticut

This book is dedicated to
Lucille (Grandma) West, who bought me a sailor suit
when I was two years old. Who would have thought?!

Copyright © 1998, 1999 by Jim West

All rights reserved. No part of this book may be reproduced or transmitted in any form by an means, electronic or mechanical, including photocopying and recording, or by any information storage and retrieval system, except as may be expressly permitted by the 1976 Copyright Act or by the publisher. Requests for permission should be made in writing to The Globe Pequot Press, P.O. Box 480, Guilford, Connecticut 06437.

Cover and text design by Laura Augustine

Library of Congress Cataloging-in-Publication Data.
West, Jim, 1959–
The essential little cruise book: secrets from a cruise director for a perfect cruise vacation/Jim West.—2nd ed.
p.   cm.
ISBN 0-7627-0508-6
1. Ocean travel. 2. Cruise ships. I. Title.
G550.W47   1999
910'.2'02—dc21
99–15972
CIP

Manufactured in Quebec, Canada
Second Edition/Third Printing

Contents

Acknowledgments

I wish first to thank God for giving me so many wonderful opportunities: to explore the planet, to meet fascinating people, and to discover more about myself. My cruise adventures and life adventure have been absolutely brilliant thus far.

I thank my family: My mother and father, who taught me the value of being a good, honest, and decent person. My brothers, Michael and Ricky, and my sisters, Laurie and Marysue, who listened to my countless cruise stories with genuine interest.

I also would like to thank Richard, Gretchen, Tony, Melissa, Mark, Gayle, and Voit for their friendship. Many thanks to my colleagues at Princess Cruises, Celebrity Cruises, and Orient Lines, who gave me the opportunity to work with their companies.

I am also grateful to Sir Edmund and Lady June Hillary, to my friends at many of the other cruise lines, and especially to Cruise Lines International Association for their support in so many of my projects. Special thanks to Bret Bullock and to Ditmar Wertanzl (Crystal Cruises), who believed I could be a cruise director and then opened the door.

And finally, it is with great appreciation and fondness that I thank the half million cruise passengers I have sailed with over the years. God bless.

HELP US KEEP THIS GUIDE UP TO DATE

Every effort has been made by the author and editors to make this guide as accurate and useful as possible. However, many things can change after a book is published—establishments close, phone numbers change, facilities come under new management, etc.

We would love to hear from you concerning your experiences with this book and how you feel it could be made better and be kept up to date. While we may not be able to respond to all comments and suggestions, we'll take them to heart, and we'll also make certain to share them with the author. Please send your comments and suggestions to the following address:

The Globe Pequot Press
Reader Response/Editorial Department
P.O. Box 480
Guilford, CT 06437

Or you may e-mail us at:
editorial@globe-pequot.com

Thanks for your input, and happy travels!

I first began working on cruise ships (the original *Dawn Princess*) ten years ago. Since then I have sailed on more than six hundred cruises and have had the unique opportunity to talk with nearly one million cruise passengers, from families and seniors to single and corporate travelers. Early in my career as a cruise director, I noticed that many passengers were desperate for information that would make their cruise a success. Many of them made comments like, "If only we had known this before we left home!" or "Why didn't my travel agent prepare me for this?" The same questions and concerns arose time and again. I began to keep a journal, noting the issues and concerns that were especially important to passengers. This book evolved as a result.

Of course, no matter how good the cruise line, no one can take you by the hand and explain every last detail about a cruise. Each and every voyage is different—the officers, staff, and crew onboard the ship; the passengers sailing on that particular voyage; weather conditions; the ship itself; and how much information your travel agent has given you are all important factors in determining the success of a cruise. But, that said, it is also true that a few tips can help to smooth the cruising waters. Whether you are planning your first voyage or your tenth, the tips and suggestions provided here can make the difference between having a good cruise and having an excellent cruise.

Since writing the first edition of this book, I have noticed many changes in the cruise industry. More and more people are discovering that a cruise is the best vacation value for their money, and with more and more ships being built in the next couple of years, the cruise lines are looking for ways to fill them. As a result, passengers can find great prices on cruises anywhere around the world. They can sail on brand-new cruise ships that are more like floating resorts than hotels. Many have interactive television systems, more appealing menu options, and more attractive ports of call. Some have inside cabins with a window facing the atrium lobby of the ship, and some even are time-share vessels so you can own the cabin in which you stay.

It's often heard that a cruise is what you make it. You'll be presented with an opportunity to activate your aliveness, so let your senses run wild!

THE ESSENTIAL
LITTLE CRUISE BOOK

FIRST THINGS FIRST: CHOOSING A CRUISE

*M*illions of people dream about taking a cruise—and with good reason. Cruise lines offer an exciting array of cruise "products" today, and it takes only the skilled juggling of a travel planner to match your personality and budget with the cruise line, cruise ship, and itinerary that suit your needs. One of the most important things to remember when planning your cruise is to gather as much information as you can *before* you reach into your wallet and dish out money. Having the right information beforehand will prevent problems from occurring and eliminate unpleasant surprises once you arrive onboard the ship.

Cruise ships are often referred to as "floating resorts" or "floating hotels," since your life is centered on the vessel for the duration of the cruise. Thus, it's essential that you become familiar with the amenities

4 that a particular ship and cruise line have to offer. You won't want to be booked on a cruise with a family-oriented theme if you are single and looking to party hearty. If you hate sunny, hot weather, you'll be happier cruising to Alaska than to the Caribbean. And if you don't like crowds or glitz, a freighter that accommodates only twelve passengers may please you more than a huge, modern cruise ship that draws a couple of thousand.

DOING YOUR HOMEWORK

Think of preparing for your cruise as if you were preparing for a test at school. You can do just enough work to make a passing grade, or you can do a more thorough research job and score an A+—which translates into an excellent vacation!

The best sources of information about cruising are cruise travel agents, friends and family who have gone on cruises, travel books and magazines, and the Internet. Ask questions and keep notes about what you learn.

When preparing for your cruise, get as much information in writing as possible, such as promises from travel
agents and cruise lines. This will protect you in the
event a dispute occurs.

Read information identifying shore excursions that will
suit your taste and budget. A list of the excursions can
be obtained from the cruise line, through your travel
agent, and on the Internet.

Many cruise lines and travel agencies have their own
Web sites. Browse the Internet for specials and information, then contact your travel agent and share what
you've learned.

Ask your travel agent to order a videotape of the
cruise you are considering. This will help you decide if
the ship, itinerary, and style of the cruise line suit your
vacation needs.

Porthole Magazine (954–746–5554), *Cruise Travel
Magazine* (847–491–6440), *Cruise Industry News*

6 (212–986–1025), and *Travel Weekly* (800–360–0015) are great sources of information on the cruise industry.

Cruise books and magazines are certainly helpful, but probably the best source of information is someone who has actually been on the same cruise you are planning. Ask your travel agent for names of people in your community who have cruised on the same ship or have traveled to the same destinations.

To obtain a free subscription to *Cruise and Vacation Views,* a bimonthly magazine about the latest trends, discounts, itineraries, and industry news, call toll-free (888) 876–8600 and ask for the subscription department.

An organization called Cruise Lines International Association (CLIA) represents the entire cruise industry. To receive the latest, up-to-date information about the industry, and to have your basic cruise questions answered, call (212) 921–0066 for a brochure.

WHERE TO GO?

One of the questions that I am asked most often is, "Where is the best place to cruise?" My standard answer? "Cruise anywhere, anytime, anyplace! Your worst day on a cruise ship is better than your best day at work!"

As we enter a new millennium, cruise passengers are becoming more adventurous about exploring Planet Earth. Now that more and more people are testing the cruising waters, cruise lines have become enthusiastic about sailing to new and exciting ports of call. The Mediterranean Sea, Baltic Sea, Canary Islands, Red Sea, Indian Ocean, Southeast Asia, Amazon River, the South Seas, and even Antarctica are quickly becoming popular cruise areas. Who would have thought even twenty years ago that you could explore so many remote areas of the world in comfort and luxury, and at such affordable prices?

There are a number of cruise lines operating in all different parts of the world. For space reasons, however, I cannot list them here. Your travel agent (especially an agent that specializes in cruise travel) is the best source of information on which lines sail to which regions.

8   When planning a cruise to Alaska, remember that the weather is always unpredictable. It can rain any day and every day, whether you cruise in May, July, or September. The middle of the summer is not necessarily the best time to see Alaska, contrary to what some agents may suggest: The weather may be extremely hot; there will be up to six cruise ships in the same port of call at the same time (15,000 passengers walking around); and the price is higher than at any other time of the year.

Check with your local library or bookstore for general information and the history of the ports of call your ship will be visiting. You will have a better understanding and appreciation of each locale when the ship docks and you begin exploring.

On your Internet browser, type in *cruising, cruises,* or *cruise lines* and you may find specific information regarding the ports of call you plan to visit. You may even try to communicate with people in that area of the world in one of the chat rooms.

The people you meet in the different ports of call are one of the things that you will remember about your vacation. Cruise in an area where the people have a reputation for being friendly and polite to tourists.

A cruise that stops at more ports of call does not necessarily mean a better cruise. Keep in mind that an endless round of ports can become tedious. And many passengers enjoy being at sea as much as, if not more than, being on land.

Unless you have been on a number of cruises and proved to have exceptional stamina, look for a cruise itinerary that is not too demanding, especially if you are not able to walk around easily.

SIZE MATTERS!

Like people, cruise ships come in all sorts of shapes and sizes. Some are classy, with sleek lines, while others are somewhat brassy. Some are huge and a bit show-offish, some very romantic and intimate, and others just efficient and functional. A larger ship is not necessarily a better ship—and vice versa. Your personal preferences as to size and other defining characteristics of a ship, such as age, should dictate your choice.

Think of a large ship as a floating resort and a small ship as a floating inn or hotel.

The smaller the ship, the more intimate the surroundings and personalized the service on the cruise. It is also likely to be more expensive. These types of cruises tend to attract older and more sophisticated travelers.

Smaller ships provide quick and easy disembarkation when the ship is docked in port, not to mention on the final day of the cruise.

Generally speaking, the smaller the ship, the more the cruise line has focused on the ports of call and shore excursion program.

The promenade deck on a larger cruise ship completely wraps around the ship, whereas the promenade deck on a smaller vessel may wrap around only three sides.

Larger vessels, for the most part, have more people, more noise, and more activities.

The larger cruise ships provide a greater assortment of activities and entertainment for passengers of all ages.

Generally speaking, the larger the ship, the more lavish the production shows, casino, swimming pools, health club and spa, and sunbathing areas.

The larger the ship, the greater the chance that you will be tendered ashore in smaller boats.

Sometimes the size of the ship is less important than the age of the ship. New ships offer the latest technology, with conference rooms and computers that are connected to the Internet, interactive television, enormous playrooms for children, and state of the art health and beauty facilities. The cabins are fresh and

12 more attractive, and the shower stalls are comfortably sized. The public rooms provide more space, and the entire ship is made to accommodate large groups of people. Nearly all of the major lounges are wheelchair accessible, and the ships boast more sophisticated safety systems.

Many older ships have larger cabins with more closet and drawer space. These ships can withstand a storm better than some newer ships because they were constructed with deeper drafts. There are usually more intimate spaces available in the public areas, and there are more classic nautical lines and wood inlays, as opposed to neon lights and water slides.

The maiden voyage of a cruise ship is very exciting, but problems are inevitable. Don't expect everything to be perfect. As with all things that are brand new, it takes some time before the kinks are worked out.

TYPES OF CRUISES

The cruise industry, more than any other segment of the

travel industry, boasts a nearly endless variety of options for travelers. When they hear the word cruise, most people immediately think of coastal voyages. But there are also riverboat and river barge trips, round-the-world cruises, tall sailing-ship cruises, freighter and cargo-ship cruises crossing from one continent to another, and special expedition cruises. While they are all different, each of these specialty cruises offers a great opportunity for vacationing on a ship.

Some cruise lines offer a one- or two-day cruise to the "land of infinity." In other words, the ship stays at sea the entire time while the passengers enjoy the amenities of the ship.

Special educational cruises are available through some cruise lines. How about traveling to the Galapagos with a team of biologists and oceanographers? Or cruising to ports in Greece and Turkey with a group of archaeologists? Not only will you get to visit exotic places, but you will learn a great deal as well.

A cruise through the Panama Canal is not only educa-

14 tional but will also give you the opportunity to cruise in both the Caribbean and Pacific on the same voyage. And you can get a great price if it's a repositioning cruise from the Caribbean and Alaska.

Many cruise ships sail to their own private islands. These are wonderful places to just lie on the beach and relax. Look for this special option in cruise itineraries.

A trans-Atlantic cruise is a seafaring adventure, and one that is quite reasonable in price. (Before undertaking this particular kind of cruise, however, make sure you have your sea legs.) Trans-Atlantic voyages involve five to eight days at sea with no ports of call.

River barge cruises are ideal for people who are afraid of the ocean, are afraid of getting seasick, or prefer a less hurried vacation.

Don't think of a barge cruise as sailing on a tugboat. Many river barges are luxurious floating hotels, complete with elegant china, rich wood paneling, hot tubs, sauna, goose-down beds, and even fireplaces.

The obvious difference between cruising on a cruise ship and cruising on a river barge is the body of water on which you travel. A barge will cruise down charming narrow waterways and through canals and enter areas of the world that cruise ships could never reach.

If you're interested in cruising on a river barge, contact River Barge Excursions for a free copy of their brochure. They provide wonderful rates and diverse itineraries throughout the United States. For more information call toll-free 888-GO-BARGE or try their Web site at www.riverbarge.com.

Cargo ships are very informal, so you do not need to pack any formal wear. One of the nice parts of cruising on a cargo ship is the constant interaction between the passengers and the officers onboard.

You will not find many organized activities on a cargo ship or freighter. It is a great place to write a book, meditate, or just sit back and soak up the sun.

Passengers on a cargo ship are more relaxed, more flexible, and usually have more time to cruise.

A world cruise is one of the most prestigious adventures of all. These cruises often last for months, and the cost can easily reach $100,000 per person. The lines that offer world cruises also allow passengers to book just one portion or section of the cruise—a good way to meet fascinating seasoned travelers at a fraction of the time and cost of a true world cruise.

You may enjoy taking a theme cruise—perhaps one with sports celebrities, country western stars, jazz musicians, or even one that features rock oldies. Contact your cruise travel agent for a list and the dates of these cruises.

If you are an active person, a cruise onboard a sailing cruise ship may be just the ticket. Even though these ships are engine-powered for the most part, the computerized sails are used from time to time. These ships typically travel to more remote places and offer exceptional shore adventure programs.

Planning a cruise as part of a fund-raising effort is a great way to raise additional funds for your organization or company. Contact a company called Cruise Fund-Raising Inc., PO Box 147, Spring Valley, IL 61362 with your request.

The most fascinating and educational trips are the expedition and nature cruises. These provide a hands-on experience with wildlife, the environment, and the sea. The prices for these cruises are higher than for most other types, but they are well worth the investment for those with adventurous spirits.

DETAILS, DETAILS: PLANNING THE TRIP

OK. You have thought about what part of the world you want to cruise in, the size of ship that appeals to you, and what type of cruise suits your needs and interests. Now it's time to start putting together the details that will form the basis of your wonderful cruise vacation.

THE PERFECT TRAVEL AGENT

The basic element in a good cruise experience is having a good cruise travel agent. In planning a cruise, the right agent can save you literally hundreds of dollars, if not thousands. Forget riffling through the Sunday travel section of the newspaper and signing up directly with a cruise line that advertises a tempting bottom line (there are usually many restrictions and hidden costs). You need a cruise expert to arrange the cruise that's right for you.

The perfect cruise travel agent is one who has been on more than a dozen cruises, one who will not accept the

20 first price offered by a cruise line, one who has sailed with more than one cruise line, and one who provides more information than you ever thought possible.

✳

I highly recommend that you select a cruise professional. Even if your regular travel agent is not familiar with cruising, he may say that he can find the best cruise for you, thinking he might lose you as a client. Assure him that you will continue to use him for other travel arrangements in the future or when he has more experience with the cruise industry—and contact an expert. You'll be glad you did.

✳

To determine if an agent is qualified to plan your cruise, ask a few pivotal questions: How many cruises have you personally been on? What makes you special as a cruise travel agent? Why do you feel you can provide a better cruise package than the competition? What cruise lines do you work with on a regular basis, and why? How many years have you been involved in the cruise industry?

✳

Word of mouth is a great way to find a good cruise travel agent. Ask your friends, family, even business associates if they have any recommendations.

When considering working with a cruise travel agent, ask her for the names of several cruise clients who have used her services in the past. If she is reluctant to give you this information or makes any excuses, look for another agent.

Your dealings with a cruise travel agent should be fun—your relationship sets the tone for your vacation. If your personalities don't click early on, it's best to find another agent.

If the travel agent you have chosen is insistent on one particular cruise line and does not offer any other suggestions, it may be that he receives a higher commission from that particular cruise line. Ask the agent to give you information about two or three other cruise lines offering the same kind of product and

22 price. If he doesn't seem enthusiastic, consider moving on to another agent who is interested in *your* needs rather than the commission.

A good travel agent wants to do everything possible to plan the best cruise vacation for you, so give as much information as you possibly can. Be specific about how much money you are willing to spend, where you want to go, how long you want to travel, whether you want a quiet, relaxing cruise or an active one, and so on. In other words, do your homework before you walk into the travel agency.

Ask your travel agent to arrange the details for a special-occasion cruise. I can't think of a better place to celebrate a birthday, anniversary, graduation, family reunion, or maybe just the fact that you have enough sense to celebrate life! Cruise lines are very happy to accommodate any special requests, within reason.

Your travel agent can help you arrange to renew your wedding vows onboard the ship. (If you feel impassioned once onboard, the cruise director may also be able to assist you!) Many cruise ships now have an onboard wedding chapel. If you would like to get married onboard a ship, your travel agent can arrange the ceremony through the cruise line's special wedding department. There is usually a $1,000 price tag for a basic wedding onboard the ship.

Good travel agents are worth their weight in gold. Once you've found one, show your appreciation with compliments or thank-you notes.

QUALIFICATIONS TO LOOK FOR IN AN AGENT AND AGENCY

The way an agent and agency present themselves is exactly the way they will handle your travel requests. Does your agent look sloppy and lack energy and details, or is she sharp and tailored, full of energy and a sense of humor? Is the agency cluttered, disorganized, with tatty, sun-bleached cruise-ship displays in the window, or does it look tidy and busy, with happy employees and customers?

24   Look for the CLIA (Cruise Lines International Association), ASTA (American Society of Travel Agents), NACOA (National Association of Cruise Oriented Agencies), or ARTA (Association of Retail Travel Agents) emblem on the front door or window of the travel agency. This means that it is a legitimate agency.

If a travel agency in your area is aggressive in its promotions and advertising, chances are it will be just as vigorous in finding you the best deal.

Some travel agencies place advertisements in newspapers or magazines, claiming to be the exclusive representative for a particular cruise line. Don't be fooled by these ads. No cruise line is exclusive to one travel agency.

SELECTING YOUR CABIN

Even if you expect to use your cabin just as a way station—breezing in and out to catch a few z's and to shower—choosing the right one for you is an important

part of planning your cruise. Your selection will affect not
only the price but also the general tone of your adventure.

Think small. In fact, think very small. Don't expect your cabin to be as spacious as those pictured in cruise-line brochures. (When they shoot the cabins for brochures, photographers often use angle lenses that make them look larger than they are.)

View your cabin as you would your bedroom. How big and fancy does it need to be? If the bare essentials of space and amenities will do, ask your travel agent to look for lower-cost options. If you typically enjoy spending time in your hotel room as much as any other part of a vacation, allocate a larger portion of your budget to a more luxurious cabin.

Ask your travel agent to inquire about the drawer space, wardrobe space, and bathroom facilities in the cabin you are thinking of booking. If you know the actual dimensions, you won't be unpleasantly surprised when you get on the ship.

26 If you book an outside cabin with a window (typically more expensive than an inside cabin), have your travel agent check the ship layout to make sure that a lifeboat does not block the view—unless, of course, you willingly receive a discount on the cabin.

Generally, the hotel manager onboard the ship decides who is allowed to get a complimentary cabin upgrade. If you are requesting such an upgrade, remember that a special note accompanied by a nice bottle of wine could suddenly find you in a plush new environment. There are no guarantees, but it's worth a try!

If you get onboard the ship and decide that you want an outside cabin instead of the inside cabin you booked, or you want a verandah instead of just a window, contact the information desk and ask if anything is available. You will have to pay for this cabin upgrade, but it will be worth it.

On many of the newer ships, the cabin size is the same whether you are on the fifth deck or the ninth (excluding the suites, of course). Why pay more for a higher deck, which will increase your chances of getting seasick?

Beds onboard a ship are called berths. Some berths are side by side, and some are upper and lower. Ask your travel agent to find out exactly where these berths are located in the cabin. Honeymoon couples and those seeking a little romance will not be too happy if the twin beds are bolted to the floor!

Avoid booking your cabin above or below the disco or above the propellers. There is a considerable amount of noise and vibration in these cabins.

If you can afford it, book a suite with a private verandah. You'll have delicious privacy while lying in the sun, viewing the scenery, and enjoying a private dinner.

Most cruise ships provide a shower facility, not a bathtub, in a standard cabin.

28 When money is no object, you might consider booking the penthouse suite on an upscale cruise line
rather than a regular suite on a luxury line. This will
give you your own personal cabin steward, butler, maid
service, and plenty of luxurious extras.

DISCOUNTS AND UPGRADES

*When you are planning your cruise, remember that there
are always ways to get a better fare than the first one
quoted. Ask your travel agent to really dig to find the best
possible price. More times than not, the agent can receive
a discount or cabin upgrade for you simply by asking the
district sales manager of the cruise line for help.*

Passengers who frequently cruise with a particular line,
people celebrating a special occasion, travel agents,
and travel-club members often receive a free
upgrade—if space is available. Inquire about this at the
information desk once you are onboard. If you are told
that all of the cabins are taken, don't argue.

If you have cruised in the past with a particular cruise

line and are planning to book another cruise with the same company, ask your travel agent to inquire about a free category upgrade for your next cruise. Cruise lines may accommodate such requests, providing the ship has available cabin space.

Cruise lines frequently offer two-for-one deals. If you come across any bargain rates—written or announced—ask your travel agent to investigate. These deals are restricted to certain dates and ships, and a two-for-one rate is quoted from the prices listed in the brochure. Quite often these rates are *more* than what a last minute discount would be.

Many cruise lines offer a discount for a third or fourth person traveling in your party, provided you all stay in the same cabin.

Cruise for free! Organize a group of sixteen people or more, and you can cruise for free. Your travel agent can give you more information.

30   If you're interested in starting a cruise business of your own, contact Cruise Concepts Inc. Their in-house cruise agency program will give you an opportunity to work out of your home and have the advantages of receiving high commissions for selling cruises. Call toll-free (888) 876–8600 for more information.

Some cruise lines allow children to cruise for free as long as they are staying in the same cabin as two adults who are paying a full cruise fare.

Cruise lines offer substantial discounts on their "repositioning cruises"—when a cruise ship is being moved, or repositioned, from one area of the world to another. The most common months for this are April and October.

Some cruise lines now offer the opportunity to charge your entire cruise vacation to a credit card provided by the cruise line. You are then allowed two to three years to pay for the entire vacation. Be careful, however, as the interest rates for these cards can be sky-high.

Sometimes cruise lines offer promotional rates to single cruisers if they book at the last minute. Your travel agent should receive this information periodically.

If you book your cruise a year in advance, you could receive a substantial discount. You will also be one of the first passengers considered if and when the ship offers any free cabin upgrades.

Cruise lines will occasionally offer a very low discounted price on a cruise a week or so before the ship departs. (If you have already purchased your ticket and the price of the discount is considerably less, it is unlikely you will be eligible for a refund.)

A back-to-back cruise is a combination of two consecutive cruises combined into one long one. Some cruise lines offer a substantial discount if you book this kind of trip.

Compare prices! There are many cruise agencies that buy a great number of cabins from cruise lines at a

32 substantial discount. These cruise warehouses pass along excellent savings to their cruise clients. For more information about discounted cruises, call toll-free (800) 708–0880 and compare prices.

If the cruise line terminates your cruise midway through the voyage due to mechanical problems, health concerns, and so on, it may be responsible for providing you with a full refund. In most cases, the refund will be made through your travel agent.

BOOKING THE CRUISE

Booking the cruise is the first big step to your adventure. Make sure you have all the information beforehand—in writing—so that you feel comfortable paying your deposit.

Give your travel agent ample time to find the best price and the best ship for you. It takes a little extra effort to design a good cruise package.

If you fear that you might be claustrophobic or afraid of the water, plan a one- or two-day cruise to see if you are able to tolerate the water and the surroundings. Most likely, there will be no problem.

If possible, book a one- or two-day prepackage before your cruise. That way you have a couple days to enjoy your port of embarkation before departure. It also allows time for any lost luggage to catch up with you.

Read all of the fine print in the "terms" portion of the cruise ticket before paying for your cruise. If there is anything you do not understand, have your travel agent explain it to you until it all makes sense.

It may be tempting to book your cruise directly with a cruise line, either by telephone or through the Internet. Be aware there are very few people, if any, who will be available to assist you if something should go wrong. Book your cruise through a cruise travel agent. They will not only defend you if there is a problem, but they can use the leverage of their cruise business to get immediate customer satisfaction.

34   If possible, pay for your cruise with a credit card. If any problems arise, the credit-card company can assist in sorting out the situation.

✴

Even if you have already placed your cruise deposit with a travel agent, if a better deal comes along with another agent or through a cruise warehouse for the exact same cruise, you *can* cancel your reservation with the original agent. But first make sure you are not under any penalty restrictions and that you have investigated the situation thoroughly.

✴

Port charges are added to the cost of the cruise and will be reflected in your cruise ticket. These typically are about $50 to $200 per person, depending on the itinerary.

✴

If a two category cabin upgrade is offered when you are booking your cruise, it may not be a better location than the original category or the one just above it. A midship cabin in a lower cabin category is preferable to a higher category cabin toward the front of the ship or above a noisy lounge.

When cruising to very special places, such as Alaska, consider booking a land package to precede or follow your cruise. It will add another dimension to your experience in this region.

If you book your own air transportation to the ship, be sure not to book a return flight before 12:30 P.M. If the disembarkation process is slow or delayed, you may miss your flight, and the cruise line will not be responsible for helping you reschedule another.

Air-sea packages give passengers free transfers to and from the ship. If you have not purchased one of these packages, you may still purchase a transfer coupon to be used on the day you embark onto the ship and the day you disembark to go home.

Most cruise lines offer some type of cancellation insurance policy that will provide a full refund should you have to cancel your cruise. This price is usually higher than most other travel insurance policies. When pur-

36 chasing cruise insurance, call (815) 663–3100 and ask for a free Access America insurance form.

TO INSURE, OR NOT TO INSURE?

I always advise people to pay the extra money for cruise insurance, especially if they are over age fifty. Life is full of surprises, and sometimes people simply must postpone their vacation. It is well worth the relatively small insurance fee to guarantee a refund in such cases.

Some insurance policies will cover emergency medical evacuations from the ship, lost baggage, a delay in the departure date, or even interruption or cancellation of the cruise. Be very clear on what type of coverage you buy. Get everything in writing, and review the fine print carefully.

Most cruise lines offer some type of cancellation insurance policy that will provide a full refund should you have to cancel your cruise.

If you decide to cancel your cruise, you will receive a

full credit only if you submit your notice in writing no later than two months prior to the day the ship departs. During holidays, this notice must be received in writing by the cruise line three months in advance.

❄

Some travel-insurance companies have an exclusive family plan in which children sixteen years and younger receive full coverage at no additional charge, when accompanied by adults who purchase the policy.

❄

You never know what type of medical emergency could occur on your vacation. Buy insurance that covers a medical emergency evacuation from the ship.

ON THE
ROAD TO THE
HIGH SEAS

*T*here's something about going to sea that makes people feel like they have to be more prepared than when they travel on land (or, for that matter, in the air). In actuality, the steps toward embarking on your cruise are much the same as going on any vacation. That said, however, it is also true that knowing what to expect and being well prepared will make your cruise that much more pleasant.

WHAT TO BRING?

They say that half the fun of going on a vacation is anticipating and planning it. Preparing your wardrobe and packing for the cruise are part of that fun. The bottom line: Don't get carried away! (Typically, first-time cruisers pack at least twice as many clothes as they need.) One or two bathing suits, a couple of shorts and shirts, a few sets of nice casual wear, and a couple of more dressy outfits should work out just fine.

40   *If you feel that you've underpacked (a rare occurrence), you can always pick up something wonderful in the shops onboard the ship or in a port of call.*

Don't overpack, don't overpack, don't overpack! Think in terms of essentials. Save room for the stuff you'll be buying (inevitably) on your trip.

When taking a seven-day cruise, don't pack more than one piece of luggage and one carry-on bag. Less is better.

Be aware that the airlines are enforcing their carry-on luggage policy, so be sure your travel agent has provided information regarding the size of your bags. Again, less is always better.

Once you finalize your list of things to take, stick to it. Too often people develop a superb list, only to ignore it during the actual packing. Caught up in the heat of the moment, they start tossing things into the suitcase with abandon. Usually these items are never used on the vacation.

A good packing rule to remember when going on a cruise: When in doubt, leave it out!

Bring an attractive cover-up that will carry you elegantly from pool to cabin. In fact, when choosing all of your wardrobe, go for classy rather than gaudy. It won't cost any more, and you'll look better!

Bring a backpack. You can use it as carry-on luggage to and from the ship, and it will be handy both on the ship and on shore excursions.

Pack workout gear if you plan to take advantage of the health-club facilities onboard.

Most cruises provide a mix of casual, informal, and formal evenings. Ask your travel agent to find out from the cruise line what mix your voyage will offer so you can plan your wardrobe accordingly.

✺

On most cruise ships, the formal dress code for men requires a suit or tuxedo.

✺

Dressing for formal evenings has been made easier for men by a company called Floating Formals. This company will deliver your tuxedo to your cruise ship and collect it when your cruise is finished. For more information call 800–833–5621 or locate them on their Web site www.floatingformals.com.

✺

While most cruise ships offer dry cleaning, opt for washable items whenever possible. Who needs the hassle and expense of dry cleaning on vacation?

✺

People often get carried away when it comes to shoes, which take up a lot of luggage space. Try to bring just one pair of walking shoes, one pair of versatile casual shoes, and one pair of dressy shoes. (You certainly know a cruise is not the time to break in a new pair of shoes.)

Pack some moisturized wipes. They will always come in handy, especially when cruising with children and while on shore excursions.

✺

Because of the variety of food offered onboard the ship, you may be tempted to try different types of spicy foods for the first time. Pack an antacid, just in case!

✺

A cruise is a great place to show off jewelry, especially on formal evenings, but don't bring anything that you could not bear losing, such as family heirlooms. Cubic zirconia is the way to go.

✺

On a cruise, women can get a lot of use out of leggings. Not only can they be dressed up or down very easily, but they can also be hand-washed.

✺

Cruise lines do not encourage passengers to pack an iron, so the best clothing for a cruise is wrinkle-free. Travel Smith, one of the leading distributors of travel clothing, offers a variety of wrinkle-free, easy-to-pack

44 garments that can be worn for daytime casual or nighttime dress-up. For a free copy of their catalog, call toll-free (800) 950–1600. (Mention code CR 19915 and you'll receive an extra 10 percent discount!)

Bring a night light to place in the bathroom or a small flashlight for use in the middle of the night. This will be especially useful for passengers with inside cabins.

If you are traveling with a child who wets the bed, pack a plastic sheet to protect the ship's berth.

Carry some business cards. You never know what kind of contacts you will make among your fellow passengers.

Pack a small pair of binoculars, especially if you are cruising to an area where you will be looking at wildlife. If you wear glasses or contact lenses or take prescription medicine, pack extras, along in your carry-on bags.

Pack clothing with elastic waistbands. You will feel more comfortable at the end of the cruise, when it is likely you will have gained a pound or two . . . or five!

❄

Don't bring more than a couple T-shirts. You will probably buy some in the ports of call or in the shops onboard the ship.

❄

Surely you won't forget to bring sunblock or sunscreen!

❄

Toss in a highlighter marker so that you can easily mark the activities on the daily program that interest you.

❄

Pack a small first-aid kit to take with you on your shore excursions. This will help if you have a minor injury and do not want to pay for treatment at the medical facility onboard the ship.

❄

Bring insect repellent if mosquitoes or other pesky insects lurk in the ports of call you will be visiting or if you are sailing on a river cruise.

46 If you will be cruising in an area that is warm or hot, pack lightweight, loose-fitting clothes that can be easily washed and dried.

If you will be visiting an area that is cold, pack a warm coat with a lining that can be easily removed.

If you are cruising in an area where the local residents speak a foreign language, pack a small phrase book and memorize some key phrases.

Men will find nylon swim shorts with pockets to be very versatile. They can be used as walking shorts, and they dry quickly.

Pack some toiletries and a change of clothing in one of your carry-on bags. In the event your check-in luggage is lost or stolen and does not arrive at the ship, you will have some essentials to keep you fresh for a couple of days.

For stylish and affordable cruisewear with a nautical look, contact Ultra Blue, a Smallwoods yachtwear boutique. Call (954) 525–BLUE for more information. To receive a free copy of Smallwoods uniform catalogue, call toll-free (800) 771–2283. You'll look smashing and feel great!

Pack a copy of your living will when cruising in different areas of the world. Unfortunately a cruise vacation is not immune to fatal circumstances.

Bring an umbrella to protect you from rain, snow, or sun.

Pack a hat, pack a hat, pack a hat!

Invest in a good pair of sunglasses. Even in frigid regions, the glare from the sun can be intense onboard.

Even though most cruise ships provide a wake-up service, pack a battery-run alarm clock. (P.S. Don't forget extra batteries.)

48 Although every effort is made to keep you comfortable inside the ship, the air-conditioning can get too cool in some of the public lounges. Pack a sweater or jacket, preferably versatile enough in style to carry you from day to night.

When flying from a very cold climate to a very warm point of embarkation, pack your coat in your luggage just before you check it in with the airline agent.

I have to say it again: Don't overpack!

HOW TO PACK

Packing well may be an art form, but there's nothing mysterious about it. These tips will help you organize your belongings to minimize clutter and wrinkling, and to allow for easy "loading" and "off-loading" both before and after your trip.

Pack your liquid toiletry items in sealable plastic bags, and place these bags in another sealed plastic container. This is double protection against damaging your clothing or other items in your suitcase. Also make sure these containers are not filled to the top.

Place the heaviest items on the bottom of your suitcase and the lighter items on top.

Protect your clothing from shoe polish by slipping each of your shoes into an old sock or a plastic bag.

Fold shirts and blouses by making the crease below the waistline. This will help prevent wrinkle lines across the areas that show.

Packing light is the best revenge. If you can manage to pack all of your belongings into two carry-on bags, you will save time and not risk having your luggage tampered with or lost.

When you are cruising to a place that will require you to wear a heavy coat, don't pack it, carry it instead. This is also true for boots, heavy sweaters, or anything bulky

50   that will take up a lot of room in your suitcase.

Expandable luggage will prove to be beneficial when you are bringing home the souvenirs you bought during your cruise.

Tie a closed identification tag with your name, cruise line and ship, and address and phone number (preferably those of your business, for security's sake) to the handle of each piece of luggage, including your carry-on bags.

As an additional means of identification, tape the above information to the inside of each piece of luggage in case the outside luggage tag gets torn off.

In most cases, you will be directed or personally escorted to your cabin when you embark on the ship. Your luggage may not arrive for two or three hours. Don't panic. The crew members on the ship have nearly 4,000 pieces to sort and distribute—it takes time. If the ship is ready to sail and you have not yet received your bags, contact the purser's desk or the housekeeping department to ask for assistance.

❋

If your luggage gets lost, don't let it ruin your cruise. You can purchase what you need in the onboard gift shop or in the first port of call. (Of course, you already know that irreplaceable items such as prescription medicine and all valuables should be packed in your carry-on bags.)

❋

If you are using the cruise line's air/sea program (meaning that you booked your cruise and air transportation together), your luggage will automatically be transferred to the ship from the airport. Make certain you have a cruise-line baggage tag fastened to each piece of luggage.

❋

If your air transportation is *not* part of the cruise package, you will have to collect your own luggage in the baggage claim area before transferring to the ship.

52 In the event your luggage does not arrive to the ship and the cruise line and airline are unable to find it, you may be entitled to an "onboard credit" for up to $100 in the ship's gift shop. This will allow you to buy toiletries and a few items of clothing to help you get by until the luggage is found. Contact the information desk onboard the ship for assistance. If you purchased travel insurance, you may be compensated.

Don't overpack! (I had to mention it again, just in case you hadn't gotten the message yet.)

TRAVEL DOCUMENTS

It's the packet of information that makes your adrenaline flow: your travel documents. These papers are your ticket to an exciting adventure. Your travel agent will receive them a couple of weeks before your departure date and will make sure they are in order before calling you to pick them up. Keep these documents in a safe place, and once you are onboard the ship, lock them in the safe in your cabin.

Never pack cash, traveler's checks, travel documents,

prescription medicine, or other valuable items in your check-in luggage. Keep these with you in a secure carry-on bag.

Contact your credit card company before leaving and inform them you will be charging purchases in some of the ports on your itinerary. Otherwise they may be suspicious and decline any unusual charges made in these areas.

Make two photocopies of your passport, driver's license, medical insurance card, prescriptions, airline tickets, travel agent's name and telephone number, credit-card numbers, and any other important information. Leave one copy with a family member and keep one copy of these documents with you in a safe place while you are traveling, such as in the safe in your cabin.

When cruising abroad, ask your travel agent (at least six months in advance) if you will need a vaccination or medical certificate. Some countries require these, and you do not want to leave such things to the last minute.

54 Your travel agent will let you know if you will need a passport to enter any ports of call. Obtaining a passport is easy and inexpensive. Call the United States Passport Agency to obtain information (its twenty-four hour phone number is 202–647–0518). You can also call your local courthouse for information.

NAVIGATING AIR/SEA TRANSFERS

Your house is locked up tight, mail and newspaper delivery has been stopped, and Rover has been left in the neighbor's care. Finally, you're ready to leave on your big adventure!

But before you can begin cruising, you may have to fly to the embarkation point. While it's true that transfers between airports and cruise-line terminals can be tedious, a few tips should help ease the pain.

Connecting flights have a way of making people tired. Opt for nonstop flights to your embarkation port whenever possible, even if it costs a bit more.

If your flight to meet the ship is long, wear very casual clothes on the plane. Take off your shoes and put on a thick pair of socks. You'll feel much better and arrive in better spirits.

When cruising during big holidays, arrive at the airport at least two hours before your scheduled flight. Airlines do occasionally overbook, the people who check in first have priority, and latecomers will be bumped. You don't want this to happen to you—unless, of course, you're hoping to get bumped in return for a free-flight coupon. Be sure there's enough time before your cruise begins to catch another flight.

Have your travel agent book an early enough flight so that you will not panic about missing the ship. It is advisable to fly a day prior to embarking onto the ship. When you get off of the airplane, you will be greeted by a cruise line representative, either at the gate or in the baggage claim area. Have your transfer vouchers ready to give to them. The representative will tell you

56 what to do and where to go.

If you are staying at a hotel the night before you are scheduled to join the ship, ask your travel agent to confirm there will be ground transportation from the airport to the hotel and to the ship the following day. Be sure you have transfer coupons for this.

Take special care in transferring your luggage in and out of taxis and hotels, prior to embarking onto the ship. Be sure you have every piece of luggage with you before you leave these places.

If you fly to another country to meet up with the ship, you will be required to collect your luggage and pass through customs. At that point you will be instructed by the cruise line representative on where to proceed.

EMBARKATION AT LAST!

Embarkation. Even the sound of the word generates

excitement and fun. It's the start of your long-awaited vacation as you walk up the gangway to go onboard the ship. Not only are you embarking onto the ship, but you are embarking on a new adventure. Have fun!

Embarkation is a very busy time for the staff and crew members. When checking in at the cruise-ship terminal, have all of your cruise documents filled out and ready to hand to the staff. This will help to speed up the embarkation process immensely.

If you are a frequent cruiser and belong to a cruise line's repeat-passenger club, there is usually a separate check-in place for you and everyone in your party. These lines are much shorter than those for the other passengers, and you will receive VIP treatment.

After your cruise documents have been checked, you will be told where to go to walk onto the ship. There is usually a photographer standing at the entrance of the ship, ready to snap a picture of you with your windblown hair, faded makeup, wrinkled clothing, and exhausted smile. Don't worry—you can use that photograph as your "before" cruise picture.

If the ship's crew members escort you to your cabin, give them a tip. Just like hotel employees, these ladies and gentlemen are accustomed to receiving a couple of dollars for their service.

Once you have unpacked your clothing, get a small map of the ship and start exploring.

As soon as you get onboard, your cruise experience begins in a most welcome way: You will be offered a buffet meal, usually in the cafe on the top deck.

YOUR MONEY

Going on a cruise could be the best investment you'll ever make in your life. What you will spend and learn in one week on a cruise is often greater than the education you would get for a full semester at college. To get a full return

on your investment, know how to handle your money 59
while cruisin'.

Your onboard cruise card is activated by using a major credit card. This card is also used for identification when you leave and board the ship, and sometimes as the key to your stateroom. Don't forget—as with any charge card, this bill has to be paid! If you are on a budget, check your balance daily to monitor how much you are spending.

Personal checks are rarely accepted onboard a ship, so be sure you have enough traveler's checks, cash, or credit on your personal credit card to pay for your onboard purchases. Many cruise lines have ATM machines onboard (usually found near the casino) in the event you need extra cash.

Use a credit card instead of cash whenever possible. Although the bill will make your throat seize up momentarily, you'll soon realize that this approach usually provides a better exchange rate than a bank or airport booth.

60 If you are cruising in a foreign country, cruise lines will often arrange for the local bank authorities to exchange currency onboard the ship.

U.S. currency is accepted in many ports of call. Ask the purser's staff for guidance in this area.

At the end of your cruise, you will receive an itemized statement for all of your onboard purchases. After checking it over to make sure everything is correct, your charges will automatically be transferred to the credit card you used to activate your cruise card. You will not have to wait in a long line on the final night to pay your bill.

If you disagree with anything on your bill, discuss it with the purser's staff on the final night or the final morning.

Before making telephone calls from the ship, find out how much it will cost. Sometimes a call may cost up to $15 per minute! Thus, if you need to reach someone at home, wait until the ship docks in port and call from a pay telephone. If you do not have a calling card, in many cases there will be a calling booth nearby where you can buy one.

On some ships you can make calls from your own cellular phone. If it's that important for you to be easily accessible by phone, ask your local cellular dealer for details about cell phones with a "roam" feature.

When using a calling card at a pay phone that has a push-button system and you want to make more than one call, don't hang up the telephone when you have completed your call. If you press the # (pound) key after the other party has hung up the telephone, you will get another dial tone and won't be charged an additional connection fee.

THE
ESSENTIAL
LITTLE
CRUISE
BOOK

SETTLING IN

While each ship and each cruise are unique, there are certain commonalities in the world of cruising. Knowing what to expect onboard from the cruise staff and crew—and knowing what is expected of you and your fellow passengers—will enrich your vacation and the relationships you form onboard.

THE STAFF AND CREW

Most of the staff and crew are genuinely happy to have you onboard the ship, whether it's a luxury liner or a freighter. They are well trained in their jobs, and they are often very interesting people. You'll have no problem making friends among them, and you'll be glad you did.

Just ask! This is one of the best tips in the entire book. You will be amazed at how the staff and crew of cruise ships are willing to accommodate your needs.

64   If you have a waiter, busboy, or cabin steward who tells you he may get fired from the cruise line unless you give him an "excellent" rating on the comment cards, report this to the hotel manager onboard the ship. This is not true, and the cruise lines will not tolerate this type of behavior.

Don't ask the captain "Who's drivin' the boat?" when you greet him at the welcome-aboard cocktail party. Spare him—he's heard this line a thousand times.

The ship is your home away from home for a week or so. However, it is home for the crew members and staff for much longer periods. Respect the signs that say CREW ONLY. These areas are the only places they have for privacy and to take their minds off of work. Think of it this way: Would you want your customers and clients pushing their way into your living room?

The cruise staff are the fun people onboard the ship, or they should be. Whenever they are involved in an activity or event, you can expect a good time. If they ask for a volunteer to help them out, do it! You'll be glad you did.

At the end of the cruise, you will be asked to fill out a comment card. If you received particularly good service from any staff members, be sure to note their names. This is how many employees on cruise ships get their promotions and raises.

If you are going to criticize something or someone on the comment card, suggest how the problem might be solved. Cruise lines are more receptive to complaints if they are accompanied by a solution.

Get to know the staff early in the cruise. They can give you some wonderful inside information regarding the ports of call, excursions, activities, and so on.

The social hostess or concierge is usually responsible for selecting guests to sit at the captain's table for dinner. Talk with either of them if you are interested in having dinner with the captain. Usually VIPs, celebrities, passengers in the suites, frequent travelers with the cruise line, or people who present themselves as sophisticated and fun are selected for this. Sometimes passengers who have experienced an unfortunate mishap on the ship will be invited in order to smooth things over.

It is possible that you are not accustomed to having a maid service or cabin service as is provided on the ship. Do not let this intimidate you; and don't be rude or excessively demanding. These are very respectable jobs that require long hours. Be respectful and appreciative of these employees' service.

There are times when travel agents have promised that the ship will provide something but, due to circumstances beyond their control, the ship's staff and crew are unable to deliver. For example, the Jacuzzi in your suite may expire halfway through the cruise and the part to fix it won't be available for a week or so.

Unless it is a matter of life or death, let it go. Don't allow it to upset you.

TIPPING GUIDELINES

One of the questions I'm most often asked about cruising is proper tipping etiquette. It is an issue that creates a great deal of anxiety among cruisers, but a few simple guidelines will help you navigate these particular waters. Please follow the suggestions provided here and by your cruise line. What you leave these people as your gratuity for the week is important, not a favor. Be a good tipper.

Some cruise lines include tipping in the price of the cruise fare; others do not. If gratuities are not included in the fare, give what is recommended by the cruise line directly to the individuals who are supposed to receive the tip. Cruise lines will provide special tip envelopes near the end of your cruise.

If the cruise is longer than two weeks, it is customary to tip a portion of the gratuity midway through the voyage and the remainder on the last evening.

68 Many cruise lines recommend that you tip your server, busboy, and cabin steward at the end of the cruise. Find out what the policy is beforehand so that you can budget your money in advance.

The average amount of money for tips for a passenger on a one-week cruise is approximately $75—not a bad deal at all for the fabulous service provided.

It is not necessary to tip the head of a department, like the cruise director, hotel manager, purser, bar manager, chief cabin steward, or executive chef. These people make great salaries and do not expect any extra compensation for doing their job well. Buy them a drink and toast their professional talent.

Take a moment at the end of your cruise to write thank-you notes to members of the crew and staff who have really made a difference in the success of your vacation. Written words of appreciation are sometimes just as important as the cash tip.

A 15 percent tip is automatically added to the check for most of the drinks and bottles of wine that you order in the lounges. If you have been a regular customer to a particular bartender, however, leave that person some extra money on the last day of the cruise.

WHAT TO DO IF THERE IS A PROBLEM

Yes, problems can arise even on a luxurious cruise ship. If they do, take a deep breath—and then get over it! Life is too short to get stressed out about whether someone has cut in front of you while you were standing in line at the midnight buffet or whether you won that imitation-leather key ring at shuffleboard. And if the only problem you run into is the fact that your clothing has inexplicably shrunk by the end of the cruise, consider yourself a contented cruiser!

If there is a problem, gather all the facts before talking with the staff, and don't raise your voice or get hostile. If possible, back up your complaint with documentation or witnesses. If you present yourself as being civilized and level-headed, your complaint will be taken

70 very seriously. People who act like hotheads or hysterics will be viewed more skeptically.

Cruise lines are always anxious to settle disputes with unhappy passengers, providing the complaint is reasonable. The last thing a cruise company wants is bad publicity.

The staff and crew want to do everything possible to see that you have a wonderful cruise. Don't hold in your complaint until the last day, and then "let 'em have it" in the comment cards. If you do that, you'll probably have built up some resentment. Speak up early!

Present any complaint to the manager of the department where the problem occurred.

Should you encounter a problem with your cabin—for example, there is excessive noise from the generators, the category of the cabin is not what you paid for, the plumbing is not working correctly—contact the hotel manager immediately and ask to be moved to another cabin. If there are no other cabins available, ask him or her to give you written confirmation acknowledging that these problems do exist. When presented in a fair way, the cruise line may issue you a partial refund. Be sure that your travel agent follows up on this.

Most types of legal action brought against a cruise line will be heard in a federal court, as all cruise ships operate under maritime law. But this is an ordeal; try to settle any disputes out of court.

If you cannot reach an agreement with a cruise line and feel that your only alternative is to seek legal action, you must act within the deadline specified in your cruise contract. If you don't, you could forfeit your right to any case whatsoever.

If your travel agent made arrangements with the

cruise line's corporate office regarding something special for you onboard the ship, and for some reason it has not come about, talk to the hotel manager's staff. Sometimes inexperienced travel agents promise things that are impossible for the ship's staff to accommodate. Occasionally, the information from the travel agent to the office to the ship gets lost. Be patient with the onboard personnel until the problem is solved.

CRUISE ETIQUETTE

In the years that I have been cruising, I have witnessed some really remarkable things, both good and bad. Can you imagine two eighty-year-old ladies fistfighting because they wanted to dance with the same dance host at the same time? Or passengers sitting in their cabin on the last night of the cruise so they didn't have to tip their waiter and busboy in the dining room? Although some of these tips may be simple, common-sense suggestions, they serve as a reminder for those who need to brush up on their etiquette.

Don't expect everything to be perfect on your cruise!

Brace yourself; it is not going to be, even if you have spent thousands of dollars. You may encounter rough weather, a water pipe may break in your cabin, your dining-table mates might be miserable human beings. No matter what happens, go with the float—I mean flow. Have a good cruise attitude!

Laundry can pile up on a cruise, especially if there are children along. Most ships have a laundry facility on each deck. If the ship you are traveling on does not have a laundry facility and you do not want to pay to have your clothes cleaned, fill the sink in your cabin with water and add a dash of shampoo. Hang the clothes to dry on the clothesline above the shower— not draped all over the furniture.

Most cruise ships offer a selection of books in the library. If you check one out during the cruise, be sure to return it before disembarkation. (If you take it home, you may be charged.)

74 Use the right nautical terminology. The ship is called a ship—not a boat. And the port side of the ship is on the left and the starboard side is on the right. (It is easy to remember this because port and left both have four letters.) The front of the ship, or pointy end, is called the bow; the blunt end is the aft.

Elevators will be very crowded around mealtimes, before and after the evening shows, and in the morning when passengers are leaving the ship. To help ease the crunch, head for the stairs during those times, if possible.

To mail postcards and letters from the ship, take them to the reception desk. The receptionist will have them posted in the next port of call. In most cases, of course, you will have to pay the postage.

There should be complimentary stationery and post-cards in your cabin. If you do not find any, contact the information/reception desk.

When leaving your cabin, don't slam the door. Others who are staying in the cabins near yours may be sleeping or resting. Show the same consideration that you would like to receive from them.

The ship is your home for the duration of the cruise, but that doesn't mean normal civilities can be dropped. Be polite and pleasant to those around you.

Keep a grip on yourself. Getting a little tipsy and kicking up your heels on the dance floor is one thing; reeling around knocking over tables in the bar or starting an ugly argument is quite another. If you make a fool or pest of yourself because you have had too much to drink, you'll have to face the witnesses in the morning. You don't want to spend your vacation slinking around the ship, trying to avoid those people.

Be discreet with your money and personal wealth. Nobody really cares, and being ostentatious is in bad taste.

76 The ship is indeed your home away from home, but it's still a public facility. Don't wander around outside your cabin in nighties and curlers.

In the same vein, please be modest in your attire. It's not necessary for every person on the ship to become acquainted with your every bulge and curve.

Don't walk around the inside of the ship in a bathing suit without a cover-up.

If there is a long line to greet the captain at the welcome-aboard cocktail party, relax in one of the lounges until the line tapers off. You can then walk in as an individual and not as part of the herd!

To be asked to dine with the captain is an honor. Don't ever decline.

Don't drape your belongings over the deck chairs to reserve them for later. These chairs are for everyone.

Unless you are ready to use them, leave them for someone else.

Don't sit in the front row of an evening show if you are tired and could easily fall asleep after a long day of sightseeing. Others may be distracted from watching your head bob up and down. And the entertainers certainly don't want to look out and see people dozing during their act.

If you are on a cruise where the announcements are translated into three or four different languages, be patient. Sometimes the information concerns safety matters, and it is important that all the passengers understand the procedures.

If you are cruising with another person or group of people, be a good cruise companion. Don't complain or grumble about things. It will not only bring negative energy to your vacation, but you will embarrass the people with you and around you. If there's a problem, handle it quietly and privately with the cruise staff and crew; don't bore your fellow passengers with it.

Give your cabin mate some space so that you don't get on each other's nerves. Agree to participate in a few activities separately, and establish other ground rules before you embark on the cruise.

There is a reason why cruise ships do not sell gum onboard the ship. Parents, make sure your children dispose of their gum in the garbage container and not on or under the furniture.

If you have been trekking through a muddy rain forest during a tour, be considerate and do not track the mud through the ship. Take off your shoes or boots before entering the ship and carry them with you to your cabin. Once you get to your cabin, you can wash them off in the shower.

Sit at least ten rows back from the stage if you are bringing small children to the shows. If they start getting restless and talking, it will be less distracting to the rest of the audience and the performers on stage.

If the sun shines, smile. If it rains, smile and look for the rainbow.

Take a moment to commend any of the staff and crew members who you feel are doing a great job. A pat on the back goes a long way.

CRUISIN'

*D*rawing from my onboard experiences with nearly half a million people, I think I know the secret to having a really great cruise. The passengers who seem to have an absolute blast are those who have a great attitude. These people roll with the punches, are not afraid to participate in the activities, and somehow open their minds and hearts to the cruise adventure. They are nonjudgmental, a quality that allows them to be free spirits onboard the ship. Thus, to make the most of your cruise, follow this motto: Participate, don't anticipate.

BON APPETIT!

One phrase is used over and over again onboard a cruise ship: "Maybe I'll have just one more slice." Everything you have heard about the food on a cruise ship is true: It is wonderful. Don't even think about dieting while onboard the ship!

82 Have a healthy portion of baked Alaska. It is part of cruising tradition.

✳

Since meals are included in the cost, a cruise ship is a good place to try different kinds of foods. Be adventurous—you might fall in love with an entirely new kind of cuisine.

✳

Cruise ships will provide special meals for those on salt-free, sugar-free, low-fat, or diabetic diets. Your travel agent can arrange this for you in advance, or you can make arrangements with the maitre d' once you are onboard.

✳

By all means indulge in the midnight buffet, but take small plates. You'll be able to sample everything, but in smaller portions. You'll sleep better for it!

✳

A good way to placate a bulging stomach is to take a stroll on the outside deck after each meal.

Very often, table mates in the dining room start the cruise as strangers and finish as good, lifelong friends. But if you sense a personality clash early on, don't hesitate—be pleasant during the meal, and later on discreetly arrange with the headwaiter or the maitre d' to be moved to another table.

If you have had a great time with your table mates, surprise everyone with a nice bottle of champagne on the last night of the cruise and toast to a future reunion.

Cruise ships often have "open sitting" lunches. These give you an opportunity to sit with passengers other than your usual dinner companions. It's another great way to meet fellow cruisers.

Try not to eat more than five meals a day!

Don't complain at your dinner table. It will bring everyone down.

THE ESSENTIAL LITTLE CRUISE BOOK

84   When you arrive onboard, you will need to confirm
      your dining room reservations. If the ship has two sep-
      arate seatings and space is not available on the one
      you requested, contact the maitre d'. Sometimes a $10
      tip will find you in the right time and place!

                              ❋

      The barrage of cutlery at the dinner table may look
      overwhelming when you sit down to eat. Basically, the
      rule is to start with the outside silverware and work
      your way toward the plate as the courses progress.
      (Some ships offer a table-etiquette class for those who
      are really concerned about the proper use of silver-
      ware and table manners. This is not offered to insult
      anyone.)

                              ❋

      Many of the larger ships offer pizzerias and other
      venues for casual dining. These places are more desir-
      able when traveling with children or if you want a
      change from the formalities of the dining room. It is
      also a lot quicker.

                              ❋

      Tables in the dining room are designed to accommodate two, four, six, or eight people. If you are a large group or family, ask the maitre d' if you can be seated at adjoining tables.

*

Some cabins have a minibar. Just like in hotels, there is a charge for anything you eat or drink from it. All those traveling with you should be warned about this, as the cost can be substantial.

*

Do not leave food lying around in your cabin. It is a continuous battle for the cruise lines to control insects onboard their ships.

*

If you or your children are used to eating dinner at 5:30 P.M. and the first seating for dinner is at 6:30 P.M., start adjusting mealtimes at home at least two weeks prior to the cruise.

*

If your cabin has a small refrigerator, you can use it to store fruit, yogurt, or other small snacks from the buffet for later in the day.

*

If your cruise line offers a choice of seatings, consider requesting the later seating. You can stay in port longer, sleep later in the morning, and participate in more of the late-evening activities—for many people, this lifestyle is a delightful change from their normal routines.

Some cruise ships offer alternative dining areas. This gives passengers a fun option for dinner. For example, a ship might hold a "Chinese night," with a wonderful variety of Chinese cuisine, the room decorated in a Chinese theme, and the servers dressed in traditional Chinese garb. In most circumstances, reservations are required, and there may be a nominal charge.

HEALTH AND BEAUTY

Imagine sitting in a deck chair, soaking in the warm rays of the sun, as a crew member walks around the pool area spritzing you with cool mist every fifteen minutes, or lounging in the Jacuzzi before receiving an hour-long massage. Those who have been on cruises have fond memories of the pampering they received onboard.

On some cruise ships, the health and beauty facilities are among the finest in the world. Some are more than 12,000 square feet in size! You can enjoy lifting weights, taking aerobics and yoga classes, receiving nutritional advice, and getting seaweed wraps over your entire body. The facilities offer all kinds of interesting treatments, so take advantage of their services.

Make your hair and beauty appointments early in the cruise. Even if the ship is large, the days at sea are extremely busy in this department. Massages are especially popular on cruise ships, so make an appointment early. With some cruise lines these appointments can be made a couple of weeks prior to joining the ship. Ask your travel agent.

✳

Some of the massage therapists have a tendency to give a very light massage. If you prefer a deep-tissue massage, tell the attendant when you make your appointment and ask for the therapist who will accommodate your request.

✳

88 · Don't scream or shout around the pool area, and don't tolerate this behavior in your children.

If you are interested in keeping your daily workouts going, consult with the sports instructor onboard the ship to develop your own personal program to follow during the cruise.

When you get a haircut or other beauty treatment from one of the salon attendants, proper etiquette is to tip at the end of that service, as is standard practice on land.

The gym is usually very quiet when the ship is docked in port. If you don't like a lot of people around when you're working out, consider these times.

Most swimming pools are filled with filtered salt water. Use the shower facility next to the pool to rinse yourself. Also, if you used any snorkel equipment in the pool, rinse that off as well so the salt does not damage your mask or fins.

THE CASINO

Gambling is popular on most cruise ships, and the casinos can be very glamorous. As in every casino, there is always a chance to win—and lose. It can be very exciting, especially if you are one of the lucky ones cashing in a bunch of chips or yelling "Bingo!" on the last day of the cruise. Good luck!

While some ports of call have casinos, the odds of winning in them are usually poor. You'll probably have better luck on the ship.

Budget your gambling money carefully each day, unless you want to find yourself washing dishes at the end of the cruise. Take only the amount of money you are willing to lose. The best odds for winning are not walking into the casino in the first place.

When gambling on the slots, try to grab the machines that are positioned at the end of a row, in view of everyone. They usually pay off more frequently than the rest of the machines.

90 Children under eighteen years of age are not permitted to gamble in the casino.

The larger ships will have a MegaCash slot-machine area, lottery drawings, and heart-stopping bingo jackpots. Good luck!

Casino chips can be charged to your onboard credit account—but of course, at the end the cruise, you do have to pay for them!

You may get a cash advance from the casino attendants simply by presenting your onboard charge card. This amount of money will be credited to your existing account.

Ships are now so sophisticated that you can gamble right from your cabin using interactive television. Money is charged directly to your charge account, so set a limit on the amount you will spend.

ACTIVITIES AND ENTERTAINMENT

You'll never be bored on a cruise—unless you want to be. Some ships offer more than sixty activities each day! Some activities, such as art classes, are quiet and relatively solitary. Others, like organized games, are rowdy and sociable.

The great thing is, there's something for everyone. As one passenger commented, "I never thought I'd find a vacation where my husband could go and do his thing and I could do mine. It's the best vacation we've ever taken together!"

Pace yourself. Running from event to event will make you exhausted by the second day.

Take some time out to sleep in, lounge around, and kick off your shoes.

Regardless of what cabin category you have paid for, everyone has full access to the activities and events offered onboard the ship.

92   Carry a copy of the daily program so you know what time the activities are and where they are located.

✳

Many cruise ships offer vegetable-carving and ice-carving demonstrations. People who like to cook especially enjoy these, and kids find them fascinating as well.

✳

Some cruise ships offer a religious service daily, while others provide them only on holidays. Your travel agent can confirm with the cruise line whether a priest, minister, or rabbi will be onboard during your cruise.

✳

Dance classes are usually offered during the cruise. Take advantage of them, even if you do not have a partner. There's something special about dancing onboard, and there's no charge (learning on land can cost a small fortune!).

✳

Sea air makes many people especially hungry and sleepy. Take a power nap in the afternoon so that you have reserves of energy to enjoy all the wonderful things available in the evening.

The movie theater onboard the ship will be showing the latest feature films. Sometimes this room is particularly cool, so bring a sweater or shawl.

If foreign-language classes are offered, surprise your family at dinner with some of the new phrases you've learned.

Ask one of the performers in the show if they will take you backstage and show you around. Perhaps they can show you the costumes and props used in their production. It is fascinating and lots of fun.

Some ships hold a mock Kentucky Derby horse race. If you are traveling with your family or a group of friends, bid on a wooden horse. The winners receive a cash prize, and you'll have a great time dressing the horse, giving it a name, and cheering it down the track.

94 Be pleasant when you are participating in any competitive activities on the ship. Having fun—not winning—is what it's all about. Besides, a prize like a plastic water bottle is not worth getting upset over!

There is nothing like an early morning jog on the top deck of the ship to start your day. You may even want to participate in the walk-a-mile program organized by the staff.

Most activities are free, but a few are not. Be sure to ask the staff in advance if you will have to pay to participate. Trapshooting, wine tasting, and some craft activities may require a nominal fee.

Cruise lines often display elaborate artwork throughout their ships. Take time out to appreciate it. Some ships offer "tours" of the works and give a brief history of the artists.

Some cruise ships offer art auctions. If you collect

art—and even if you don't—stop by to see what is available. Many times the prices of these pieces are a fraction of gallery prices. (If they serve complimentary champagne at these auctions, be careful how much you drink. You may end up buying something you later will wish you hadn't.)

❋

If you love the entertainment, reward the performers with a standing ovation. It's not easy to sing and dance on a ship that is moving about!

❋

If you would like to sit close to the stage during the evening shows, skip dessert to arrive earlier and nab the choice seats. You can always satisfy that sweet tooth at the midnight buffet.

❋

Most engine rooms are off-limits to passengers, but you can sign up for the galley and bridge tours. Tours will give you a good look at the behind-the-scenes operations of a cruise ship. These are especially great activities for children.

❋

96 The daily program may include "Friends of Dr. Bob and Bill W." This is the code for Alcoholics Anonymous meetings. AA members should contact the cruise director if these meetings are not listed in the daily program.

Onboard guest lecturers can give you valuable information about finances, bridge playing, life enrichment, color enhancement, and umpteen more topics. These lectures are complimentary, so take advantage of them.

If the sound is too loud in a particular lounge or theater, you may be sitting in front of a speaker or monitor. The central part of the room is usually best for sound and sight lines. If the volume is really too loud, contact the cruise director to sort out the problem.

When performers ask for volunteers to come up on the stage and participate in the show, do it. You may feel silly at first, but it will be the first thing you talk about when you get home.

ONBOARD SHOPPING

Many ships offer a veritable cornucopia of shopping opportunities. There are clothing boutiques, fine jewelry stores, perfume salons, shops with souvenirs and sundries, and everything in between. In fact, you could probably out-fit yourself entirely onboard if you prefer to travel really light and bring along no luggage at all!

Most cruise lines provide duty-free specialty shops onboard their ships. (Duty-free means there are no taxes on the items.) Daily sales often sprout up, so stop in and see what is discounted each day.

Compare the prices of the merchandise sold onboard the ship with the same items sold in the ports of call. In most cases, you will find better prices onboard the ship.

Purchase some "logo wear" in the onboard shop. This is merchandise that has the name of the ship and cruise line on it. When you get home, all you have to do is wear it around and people will know you've been on a cruise.

98 If the toiletries you need are not provided in your cabin, they will probably be available in the gift shop.

Many cruise ships sell loose gemstones in one of their onboard shops. Often these offer exceptional quality and value, so take advantage of this if you plan to buy jewelry.

PHOTOGRAPHERS AND PHOTOGRAPHS

Photographs are an important part of your cruise experience. Throw all caution to the wind and snap, snap, snap. Though you might cringe when you get the bill for developing your multiple rolls of film, you'll enjoy a return on the investment for the rest of your life, as you will reminisce over the pictures again and again.

There is no obligation to purchase any of the photographs taken by the photographers onboard the ship. Give them a smile wherever they may be.

If you are traveling with a group of friends or associates, make arrangements with the ship's photographer to meet everyone in a nice area of the ship. One that has a great background, such as a grand staircase or painting, is ideal. You may even consider having this picture taken in one of the ports of call. Don't forget to ask the photographer to give you a good price.

Buy a disposable camera for each child over five years old traveling in your family, and let them take pictures throughout the cruise. When you return home, help them make a scrapbook.

Cruise-line photographers use digital cameras on most ships today. They can place any kind of background you would like to have on your pictures. Some ships are so advanced that the photos can be downloaded from the digital camera right into the television in your cabin. You can then choose which photographs you want to order from what you see on the screen.

Buy photographs in the photo gallery of you and your special someone. At the end of the cruise, have them

100 placed in a nice album and give it to your partner as a special gift. It will be cherished for years.

Buy a good camera or video recorder; you'll be glad you did.

The cruise line may provide a videographer to videotape passengers participating in various shore excursions and activities. Smile for the camera—you may just want to purchase a copy of the video before you leave the ship.

If you are traveling with your family, have a family portrait taken on one of the formal evenings. Ask the photographer to have copies made for each family member. That picture will be a wonderful reminder of your family adventure on the high seas.

Ask the photographer to take a photograph of everyone sitting at your dining table. Later, buy a copy for everyone and present it to them on the last night of the cruise.

Purchase some of the pictures taken by the ship's photographers that show some of the places and ports
you have visited during your cruise. Some of these
shots are better than the postcards you can buy from
the local shops (and undoubtedly better than the
average shutterbug's efforts).

Develop at least one roll of film onboard, if not all of
them. That way you will know whether your camera is
working correctly and whether you need some suggestions from the ship's photographers to improve
your shots.

PORTS AND SHORE EXCURSIONS

*O*ne of the things that makes a cruise so unique, so different from any other vacation, is the opportunity to explore different ports of call and to go on a wide variety of shore excursions. There are, of course, tours of these ports, by foot, car, or bus; and shopping is always fun in a new place.

Some of my fondest memories of cruises are linked to special land excursions. Imagine going on a safari in Africa, riding in a helicopter over a volcano in Hawaii, floating in a dugout canoe down the Amazon River, walking on the Great Wall of China, holding a koala in Australia, walking among the penguins in Antarctica, or traversing a glacier in Alaska. Such exciting adventures are available to passengers at an additional cost, but they are wonderful memories that will last a lifetime.

PLANNING AHEAD

Because your time is limited in each port of call, it is important to do some research and plan ahead. Don't be afraid to ask your travel agent a hundred questions, and check the Internet for additional information. What you learn can make a huge difference in the quality of your vacation.

Before leaving on the cruise, search through travel books and magazines to learn of any special festivals or holidays in the ports of call you'll be visiting.

Each country's embassy and tourism offices can provide you with valuable information about the ports of call. You can get their phone numbers by calling the information operator in most major cities.

Ask your travel agent to obtain information on the shore excursions available throughout your cruise. This will enable you to decide in advance which tours most appeal to you. (If you did not receive a booklet describing each tour from your travel agent,

collect one at the shore excursion desk on the first
day of the cruise.)

Some cruise lines offer a private club in some of the ports of call. These provide a great oasis when you are out shopping and need a relaxing place to sit and have a drink. Ask your shore excursion staff if the cruise line has such a club.

Reserve shore excursion tickets early in the cruise. The most popular tours often sell out on the first couple of days.

The newer cruise ships are designed so that you can book your shore excursions right from your own cabin, using the remote control device. You'll find operating instructions in your cabin.

When was the last time you were on a picnic? Ask the executive chef or maitre d' to organize a picnic basket for you and your companions. You'll be amazed at how relaxing and enjoyable a simple "picnic in the park" can be in a new port of call.

106 Sometimes a cruise ship is unable to dock in a particular port and the passengers are taken ashore in tender boats. The tendering operation is explained in the daily program, and most of the time the cruise director will make an announcement the night before. Be patient during the tender operations. Wait in one of the public lounges until you hear an announcement for your group to proceed to the gangway and go ashore. Passengers booked on a shore excursion are usually taken first.

It is very exciting to be outside when the ship is approaching or leaving any port of call. Walk around and take in the view.

Sometimes it is fun to stay onboard the ship when it is docked in port. The ship has an entirely different feeling when most of the passengers have left.

Be a good traveler: Learn a few key phrases—like "Please" and "Thank you"—in the language of each country you'll be visiting.

If you are returning to a port of call that you have visited in the past, don't expect everything to be the same. Explore with an open mind.

Find out as many details about the shore excursions as you can. If the staff doesn't have the answers, ask them to find out for you. This will help prevent unpleasant surprises, such as going on an excursion that involves a half-mile hike up to a waterfall—when you twisted your ankle two days before.

The shore excursion booklet provided by the cruise line includes not only a description of the tour, but also its duration and cost, as well as any other important information.

Many island ports of call have beautiful resort hotels. Consider spending the day enjoying the facilities at one of these places. In most cases, the managers of these resorts welcome cruise-ship passengers, because they know they will be spending money on food, drinks, and souvenirs. They also hope that you'll

108   return at a later date and stay at the hotel.

Some items sold in some of the more exotic ports of call are not allowed to be brought into your home country. Check with the shore excursion staff or port lecturer to learn if any items in the port of call are included on this list.

Before going into port, check the time that you must be back onboard. (Usually it is thirty minutes before sailing time.) If you miss the ship, you will be responsible for getting yourself to the next port of call to rejoin the cruise—a very expensive mistake!

In some cases, cruise lines are not legally responsible for shore excursions; the tour operators they use for some excursions are independent contractors, thereby releasing the cruise lines of any liability. If you have an accident or mishap during an organized shore excursion, the cruise lines may help, but they are not legally obligated. Make sure that your insurance covers you for situations like this.

Ask the shore excursion staff about the tipping policy in the ports you will be visiting. For example, in many places, tips for waiters are included in the restaurant check.

Be aware that people may badger you for handouts as you walk around some ports and tourist spots. If this would bother you excessively, you will probably be happier taking a guided bus or taxi tour of the port of call.

If you need to cancel a tour or shore excursion because of an illness, contact the tour office as soon as you can. In most cases, your money will be refunded, provided you have a legitimate excuse and a note from the ship's doctor.

Try to get the name and telephone number of the port agent, the number of the pier that the ship is docked at, and any other information that will help you remember the location of the ship. You don't want to find yourself on the other side of the island with no idea of how to return to the ship.

110 SHOPPING!

The expression "Shop 'til you drop" is never so true as when one is on a cruise—the gift shops onboard the ship, the wide variety of retail shops in the ports of call, the vendors on the streets selling artifacts and souvenirs! Following these tips will help your shopping budget stretch further.

If the cruise line provides one, use the recommended shopping map. If anything should break or stop working when you get home, you'll have a guarantee from the cruise line that the store will replace it. (The cruise lines receive a commission from every purchase their passengers make.)

Some ports are terrible tourist traps. Ask crew members where the real bargain places are in town.

It is easy to get caught up in the excitement of an exotic port of call. To avoid throwing your money away, follow this rule: Don't purchase anything unless you first say to yourself, "If I was walking down the street back home and saw this in the window, would I buy it?" More times than not, the answer will be no.

Before you start to buy things in the first shop you see, look around and find out what the prices are in some of the other shops. You'll be very upset if you find out the bag you paid $70 for was only $50 at the store down the street.

In many parts of the world, bargaining is a form of shopping etiquette, especially in street markets and kiosks. In these situations, never accept the first price offered. Make a counteroffer of less than half what the vendors ask, and go from there to the price you are willing to pay.

Have fun while you are bargaining. This isn't life or death! The haggling should remain a friendly exchange. If the vendor (or you) gets too pushy or heated, it's time to leave.

While it's nice to get a good deal, be reasonable, and

112 remember that people in many ports of call are extremely poor. Trying to chisel another dollar off the cost of a straw hat may mean that the vendor won't have dinner that night, while it's just pocket change to you.

Street vendors who follow you around pestering you to purchase their merchandise can best be handled with a firm "No." Avoid answering their questions and looking at them or what they are carrying.

When you walk into a shop, don't go directly to the item you want to buy or make a comment about how beautiful it is. This gives the merchant too much leverage in negotiating the price.

If you want to buy several items in one store, ask the manager to make a deal, such as 10 percent off everything.

In the more exotic ports, it is common for shop owners to give a very good deal on merchandise early in the morning. (They feel that the first sale is the most important of the day.)

When bargaining, once you decide on the price you want to pay, don't go higher. If the merchant does not accept your offer, begin to walk away. Often he will call you back and sell the merchandise at the price you quoted.

Avoid being ostentatious with your personal wealth. Do not wear expensive clothing and jewelry, and don't flash your cash around. Be discreet, not just to avoid being charged higher prices, but also to deter thieves.

Be aware: There is a tendency for shop owners to raise their prices when a cruise ship arrives in port. Always ask for a discount on the stated price.

Carry a small calculator to help you convert the exchange rate in foreign ports.

114   Buy a small piece of artwork from one of the local street vendors. For a low price, you'll have something unique that will serve as a wonderful memento back home.

In some places you can get great bargains toward the end of the tourist or cruising season. In mid-September in Alaska, for example, you can get 50 to 75 percent off the merchandise.

When you buy something that will be shipped to your home, make sure that it is packed up and the box is sealed and addressed before you leave the store. You don't want it to arrive a couple of weeks later and find that a different item has been sent, either on purpose or by mistake. Always pay with a credit card when you make purchases of this sort in case there is a dispute.

When making purchases in foreign countries using a credit card, ask the sales clerk what the rate of exchange is for that day and record it. Keep your sales receipt and compare it to your monthly credit-card statement to ensure that you have not been charged more. If there is a discrepancy, call the credit-card company to have them investigate the purchase. Avoiding this sort of problem is another reason for using the shops endorsed by the cruise line.

SIGHTSEEING AND EXCURSIONS

Face it: You're going to act like a typical tourist when you go off on your sightseeing tours. A camera will be hanging around your neck, you'll be wearing Bermuda shorts or a muu-muu and peering out from under a hat, and you'll be asking some of the same silly questions the group before asked. Even if you prefer to think of yourself as a sophisticated traveler and dress in the local garb, the people who live in the ports of call are going to take one look at you and think "tourist." Remember that everyone is a tourist outside their own country, so relax and enjoy the experience!

Treat yourself and your family to an unusual shore excursion—a helicopter ride, a submarine tour, or even a swim with the stingrays.

116 Everyone should snorkel at least once in their life. Give it a go!

Be polite to the people who live in the places you're visiting. While it's true that some may be trying to get you to buy something from them or to give them some money, other people may simply be curious about you, in the nicest possible way. Give them the benefit of the doubt.

Don't be an obnoxious foreigner. Remember that you are the guest and that the port of call is someone else's home—not your personal playground. Be respectful of the values and mores of the country.

Small children, and even most teenagers, are not particularly fond of cathedrals and museums unless it is a very quick tour. Remember this when planning your time ashore.

Use the rest room before leaving the ship. You never know when Mother Nature will call or how long it will be before you find a facility in port—or what shape it will be in!

✺

If you have a bus driver and tour guide on your excursion, proper etiquette is to tip each person a couple of dollars when the tour is complete.

✺

Don't wear beachwear in port—except on the beach. Would you wear a bikini or short-shorts while strolling down Main Street in your hometown?

✺

Ancient ruins, wineries, and old cemeteries can get boring after a couple of hours, especially if the sun is extremely hot. Remember this when you are scheduling your excursions—don't try to pack too much in, especially in the afternoon.

✺

Most city or island tours are two to three hours in length and consist of a bus ride, some shopping, and perhaps a snack. It is a great way to become familiar with the area.

✺

118 When riding on a tour bus, try to sit in the front section so you can see more easily and have a smoother ride.

If for some reason you were not happy with your shore excursion, talk (politely!) with the shore excursion manager. If your complaint is fair, you may be issued a partial refund or full credit.

Carry a small bottle of water with you in case you become thirsty. But don't drink too much, unless there is a rest room nearby.

Carry some fruit in a sealable plastic bag for the kids (they always get the munchies.) And have napkins handy to clean up any mess.

If you decide to hire a taxi for the entire day in port, you can save money if you have another couple or family ride with you. This will not only give you the opportunity to make friends with some fellow passengers, but it will also be a safer ride.

When visiting cathedrals and churches, respect the environment and keep your voice low.

Children love fish and animals. A visit to an aquarium, underwater sightseeing exhibit, wildlife park, or even a submarine ride will be a big hit.

The early morning hours offer more opportunities to see and photograph wildlife.

Collect a postcard from each port of call and make notes on the back, recalling your experience there.

If you or your traveling companions are adventurous cruisers, when the ship docks, contact the information center in the port of call for suggestions on some unusual local tours or excursions.

RENTING A CAR

Many people prefer to rent a car and explore a new spot at their own pace. It's a chance to spend some quality time with the family or your beloved and absorb the flavor of a port of call. It's a wonderful feeling of independence and relaxation.

Get a map from the rental agency and ask for clear directions to the places you want to visit—and, more important, the way back to the agency. You don't want to spend all of your time driving around in circles!

Some countries may require you to pay a fee, as much as $25, for a nonresident driver's license (typically valid for several months). Remember this expense when deciding whether renting a car is a good way to get around.

Inspect every inch of your rental car before driving it away. If you see any dents or marks, make sure they are documented in your contract; otherwise, you will be charged a very hefty sum when you return it.

Check with your credit-card company before you rent a car—your rental insurance may be covered by the company, which will save you a lot of money.

Before you drive away, make sure you have the name and telephone number of the rental agent in the event you need to call for any reason.

Ask the agent if there are any areas in town that you should avoid because of construction or crime.

Ask the car-rental agent to point out some residential areas on the maps that you can drive through. It's always interesting to check out the neighborhoods in a new port of call and see how people live.

PLAYING IT SAFE WHILE IN PORT

Concerns for safety and security are not limited to the ship. You must always take precautions whenever you step off of the ship and into another region of the world. Don't be paranoid, but do be careful and be watchful.

While swimming in the ocean or walking along the beach, wear water socks or other protective footwear. Sea urchins, rock fish, glass, and other "nasties" can be extremely painful— and sometimes deadly—if you accidentally step on them.

122   When walking around in port, especially in remote and exotic places, try to wash your hands frequently.

Drink only bottled water and other beverages, and avoid salads and other fresh vegetables.

In port, be cool—do not make political statements with your clothing. Don't wear T-shirts with religious symbols, flags, and so on.

If you go swimming, snorkeling, or scuba diving, look for posted signs that may caution you about a strong current or undertow. The excursion office onboard the ship can also advise you on safe areas to explore the underwater world.

When scuba diving or snorkeling, never place your hands in a dark hole. An eel may not be too happy having you invade its home!

If you get pricked by a sea urchin, pull the long spikes out of your skin and rub lemon or lime on the area.

The acid from these fruits will help dissolve the spikes still embedded in your skin.

If you plan a shore excursion that involves a ride in a small airplane or helicopter, ask the shore excursion staff about the safety record of the company. It is highly recommended that you book these types of excursions through the cruise line, not on your own.

Never leave valuables like a camera, watch, or Walkman unattended while you are swimming in the ocean. Ask a friend or someone you can trust to watch it for you until you return. If no one's around to assist, seal it in a plastic bag and bury it in the sand under your towel or blanket.

Don't get stranded! If you are taking a taxi to a beach on the other side of the island, make a deal with the taxi driver to come back at a certain time and bring you back to the ship. To guarantee you get picked up, agree to pay him for the entire trip (both ways) when he returns.

124 Crowded marketplaces are a haven for pickpockets and thieves. Secure your purse, wallet, and jewelry.

❉

Prepare the payment for your taxi driver while the cabby is driving; don't fumble with a bulging wallet while he looks on.

❉

When visiting areas where animals such as monkeys, birds, snakes, wild pigs, or kangaroos are not in cages, be cautious when petting or feeding them. Even if they appear to be cute and harmless, their bite or scratch could be dangerous.

❉

The ship may be docked overnight in a port. Do not walk around by yourself at night if there are not a lot of people around. Women and seniors especially should avoid walking about in the evening.

❉

When venturing off the ship, attach an identification bracelet on your child with his or her name, blood type, any chronic illness, medications, allergies, mother's or father's name, telephone number at home, and the telephone number of the ship and the cruise line.

❊

Never carry a wallet in your rear trouser pocket. It is too easy for pickpockets to steal. Keep it in a front pocket of your pants or in an interior pocket of your jacket. A money belt is recommended.

❊

Carry your identification card from the ship.

❊

Instruct your children to contact a clerk in a shop or a police officer if they get lost in port.

❊

Always lock your doors and close your windows when driving around in the ports of call—including in taxis.

HERE'S TO
YOUR HEALTH AND
WELL-BEING

*C*ruise lines take the safety and security of their passengers and crew very seriously. Follow the specific guidelines provided to you onboard, and read these tips carefully. They literally can save a life—yours.

SAFETY

They say that rules are meant to be broken, but this is one adage that definitely does not apply at sea. The safety of all people onboard a ship is paramount, and passengers are expected to abide by the rules and regulations established by the particular cruise line as well as by maritime law. I cannot stress it enough: Safety first.

Let me make one thing perfectly clear: You do not have to worry about the ship capsizing in a storm! They may be tossed around a bit, but cruise ships are built to survive the most severe weather.

The captain will not risk the lives of any passengers or crew members. Should threatening weather or political conditions crop up in a particular port or region, the itinerary of the cruise may be changed. If this happens, go with the flow. Don't grumble—such shifts in plans are made for your safety.

Look around the cabin for any objects that might pose a danger to your little tykes, such as electrical outlets, sharp furniture edges, or things that can be pulled down and hit them on the head. This is usually not a problem on newer ships, but if any hazards are found, contact the cabin steward.

Check the life jackets in your cabin. Are they properly maintained, with a whistle, proper ties, and a light (when the jacket hits salt water, the emergency light attached to the jacket automatically goes on)? Sometimes these items are missing. If this is the case, ask your cabin steward to solve the problem.

Should you detect a fire or smell smoke, don't hesi-

tate—immediately call a crew member or press the
nearest fire-alarm switch.

It is very unlikely that a person will fall overboard, but if this should happen, throw the nearest life ring into the water and contact a crew member at once.

After participating in the lifeboat drill on the first day of the cruise, look down the hallway near your cabin and locate the closest fire extinguisher and emergency call buttons.

Cabin doors are equipped with special guards or wedges to keep them from swinging open or slamming shut. Use them! You never know when the ship will suddenly list.

Never clean your pipe by banging it on the side of the ship. Burning tobacco could blow back onboard and cause a fire. For the same reason, don't throw lit cigarettes or cigars overboard. Put them out in the receptacles provided.

130 It's best to wear medium-height heels onboard rather than high heels. A sudden movement of the ship could cause you to turn your ankle and become injured.

Use the closets, not the fire sprinklers suspended from the ceiling, to hang your clothing. Garments dangling from the sprinklers could block water from extinguishing a fire in your cabin—obviously, a life-threatening situation for everyone onboard.

Always use the ship's handrails when walking outside on the deck, as a sudden motion of the ship could cause you to lose your balance.

Many doorways and thresholds on the ship have elevated ledges to cross over. Be extra careful when walking through them.

Make sure that your children know what to do if the emergency signal sounds. The instructions are posted on the back of cabin doors and all around the ship.

In the health club, take special care when using free weights 131 over your head. A sudden movement of the ship could cause you to lose your balance and drop the weights.

Never, *never* make jokes onboard about a bomb scare or a fire. As in an airport, such "jokes" will be taken seriously, and the crew is likely to hustle you to a security office for questioning. At the very least, this will be unpleasant and embarrassing. You may also be liable to a fine and criminal prosecution. Your children should also understand the serious ramifications of making these kinds of statements.

Avoid using the swimming pool if the seas are rough. The force of the waves could push you into the side of the pool and cause a very serious injury.

Do not light candles or incense while onboard. This is strictly forbidden by maritime regulations. (If there is candlelight in the dining room, it's never an open flame.)

132 Should there be an emergency, you will be told where to go. Do not push or shove other passengers, and follow the instructions given by the crew members in charge of the muster station (the place where you gather).

Do not take the elevator during an emergency situation. If for some reason it is hard for you to navigate stairs, contact the information desk and register your name and cabin number on a special emergency-assistance sheet. If something should happen, the crew will come to your cabin and help you to a safe location.

Always use caution when walking on the gangway. Do not feel pressured to walk fast just because other people are waiting behind you. Make sure each step you take is stable, and use the handrails for assistance.

Ask the cabin steward what the wattage is in your cabin or bathroom before plugging in electric razors, toothbrushes, or hair dryers. You don't want to get hurt or cause a fire. If you need a converter, the

steward will provide one. Nearly all of the newer
ships have 110-volt outlets.

It is common for black soot to blow out of the ship's smokestack. Be sure you've checked the deck chairs and lounges before you sit down on them.

SECURITY

It's unfortunate, but a fact of modern life: Cruise lines must take special precautions to ensure onboard security, from preventing theft to deterring terrorists. You can help the crew by taking the same security measures you would take on land—locking your door, not leaving your purse or wallet unattended, and so on. There's no need to be paranoid, but you should use common sense.

Passengers are not allowed to bring visitors onboard. Don't give the security staff on the gangway a hard time when they refuse to let your friends on the ship or check your identification. They are only doing their job, and it's to protect you.

134 For obvious reasons, do not bring illegal drugs onto the ship. If you are caught, you will be released to the local authorities and face criminal charges. Surely experiencing prison life in one of the ports of call is not the sort of sightseeing you have in mind!

In the event that you are harassed by a passenger or crew member, contact the hotel manager and ask for help. Cruise lines will not tolerate such behavior, and the ship's security officers will enforce this policy.

Tell children to contact the nearest crew member should they get lost onboard the ship. An announcement can be made so you can meet them at the information desk.

Lock the door each time you leave your cabin. (If you happen to lock yourself out, the purser's desk will arrange to have someone come by and open the door, or you can ask the nearest cabin steward for a hand.)

Never accept packages from strangers or bring them onto the ship, even if they say that someone is expecting it onboard.

❇

If there is a safe in your cabin, use it to secure your valuables, including your travel documents. If your cabin does not have a safe, ask at the purser's desk to use a safe-deposit box. These boxes are usually available at no extra cost.

MEDICAL CARE

A cruise ship is one place where you don't have to worry about receiving medical attention. Nearly every cruise ship afloat has a full hospital facility, including a pharmacy and X-ray machines, and a professional staff trained to take care of most medical emergencies.

If you expect to need attention from the onboard doctor, be sure you have your medical documents with you. Your travel agent should also inform the cruise line beforehand that you will be requiring medical assistance while you are onboard.

136 Tape your name and cabin number on the stems of your eyeglasses and on the inside of their cases—thus, in the event you leave them somewhere, lost-and-found will be able to reunite them with you quickly. As an extra precaution, bring a spare pair of glasses or contacts and, if possible, your prescriptions.

People who use oxygen should book direct flights whenever possible, and they should alert the onboard medical personnel as soon as they embark.

If you use the doctor's services or the hospital facility onboard the ship, you will be charged. Your medical insurance should cover this—but be sure to check with your insurance company before leaving on the cruise. Get everything in writing!

Most doctors recommend that pregnant women do not go on a cruise in their third trimester.

Keep your medicine clearly labeled, and bring along

copies of your prescriptions.   137

If you fly through several time zones on your way to joining the ship and you need to take medication at timed intervals, consult your physician or pharmacist to help you plan an easy-to-follow schedule.

Vaccinations may be required if you are traveling to exotic ports of call. Find out from your travel agent, as you will be required to show proof of your vaccination before embarking.

You can obtain a recent sanitation report of the ship you will be cruising on by contacting the Centers for Disease Control in Washington, D.C., or writing the National Center for Environmental Health, 1015 North American Way, Suite 107, Miami, FL 33132. Inspections are made at least once a year, and for a ship to be in good standing, it must score eighty-six points or higher, out of a possible one hundred.

Being on a cruise ship can motivate you to work out

in the health facility, dance the night away in the disco, or participate in an invigorating shore excursion. If you are unaccustomed to regular exercise, take it easy at first!

PREVENTING SEASICKNESS

Seasickness can really place a damper on your cruise. If you think you might be prone to motion sickness, first try a day trip onboard a ship or take a three- or four-day cruise. If you like the idea of a ship but think ocean travel might do you in, opt for a riverboat, steamboat, or barge.

Even old seadogs occasionally get seasick. Be prepared with medicine, and take precautions.

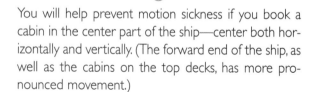

You will help prevent motion sickness if you book a cabin in the center part of the ship—center both horizontally and vertically. (The forward end of the ship, as well as the cabins on the top decks, has more pronounced movement.)

Avoid looking out the window of your cabin or of one of the lounges. The up-and-down motion can make you nauseated.

If you become seasick and your children don't, ask one of the youth counselors onboard to help keep them entertained for the day. They are usually pretty good about that.

Take an anti-seasick pill at least two hours before sailing time and throughout the cruise, if needed. If the directions on the medicine say it can cause drowsiness, take half a dose. This will allow you to enjoy the activities and entertainment without being too sleepy.

Most cruise ships are designed with stabilizers, located toward the front of the ship, that extend on both sides just below the waterline. In the event of a storm or rough seas, the stabilizers—as their name implies—help to keep the ship steady.

Some people wear a medicated patch behind their

140 ears to prevent seasickness. Ask your doctor about this option.

Pediatricians should be consulted before the cruise to provide motion-sickness tablets for the kids.

When the seas are rough, don't read a book, write postcards, or do anything else that focuses your attention downward. This may cause you to get seasick.

Old-fashioned cures that sailors have sworn by: If you do begin to feel sick, go outside immediately, take deep breaths, look at the horizon, and stay in the middle section of the ship. Also, eat some dry crackers or bread sticks, and stay away from liquids.

PREVENTING SUNBURN

Too many cruisers have spent their long-awaited vacations lying in bed in helpless torment—burned to a crisp in their zeal to get a tan. Take precautions! There are ways to get a nice glow without doing yourself in.

The sun is very deceiving on a ship. Because the breezes are blowing, keeping you cool, passengers tend to think they are not getting blasted by ultraviolet rays. Always use plenty of sunscreen or sunblock.

In the first couple of days, use a sunblock with a SPF of twenty-five or higher, and do not lie in the sun longer than an hour. You'll get a base of color, but you likely won't be scorched.

Always, always wear a hat!

Passengers have been known to get serious third-degree burns on days when the sky is cloudy. Don't let the overcast sky fool you—wear protection.

Apply sunscreen or sunblock after each dip in the pool or ocean. (Consider getting a spray for quicker application.)

Don't forget to apply sunblock on your lips, ears, and feet!

142   The beach or poolside are not the only places you have to be concerned about getting a sunburn. Put on plenty of sunblock when on a shore excursion, shopping, or strolling onboard.

If you plan to wear strapless or backless evening wear, apply sunscreen or sunblock during the day over the appropriate areas so you won't have unattractive tan lines or burns.

When cruising through the Panama Canal or other regions where the sun's rays are extremely intense, use an umbrella in addition to sunscreen or sunblock. Temperatures there can reach well over 120° F!

Antarctica cruisers must take very special care to protect themselves from ultraviolet rays, as there is a hole in the ozone layer in that region of the world.

If you go snorkeling or scuba diving, put extra sunblock on your neck, back, arms, and legs. The sun's rays can go directly through the water, so wear a T-shirt to protect your back. Believe me, you'll be grateful you did.

Use aloe vera gel or cream to relieve sunburn pain.
Products with aloe vera are also good moisturizers.

THE
ESSENTIAL
LITTLE
CRUISE
BOOK

CRUISES FOR FAMILIES AND OTHER SPECIAL GROUPS

Where can Ma and Pa Kettle and their brood, Ellen, Saab dealers, your globetrotting grandparents from London, the guys from Wayne's World, specialists in Byzantine archaeology, and the Sisters of Perpetual Hope all find the ideal vacation? On a cruise, of course! (Did you really think I'd say something else?) Virtually all kinds of groups can find a cruise that will meet the interests and needs of their members.

Cruise lines that make an effort to cater to special groups are listed throughout this chapter. Keep in mind, though, that they are not the only cruise lines that do so, and that companies regularly go in and out of business, change their focus, develop new programs and itineraries, and so on. Your cruise travel agent can get you up-to-the-minute information, but the cruise lines listed here may spark your interest.

FAMILIES

"Family vacation." Sounds like an oxymoron, doesn't it? (Think "honest politician," "military intelligence.") Those who've been there can attest that a holiday with the kids can be more trick than treat.

But families are by far the biggest "special-interest group" in the cruising industry, and no wonder; it's a wonderful way to travel as a family! Not only is it exciting and exotic, but a cruise can be amazingly inexpensive. Many cruise lines offer family discounts and packages. And the all-inclusive nature of most cruises has a valuable psychological benefit: It relieves that nagging irritation you feel when you are constantly digging into your wallet to pay for a meal—for five.

Perhaps even more appealing than the financial benefits is that cruising can be so worry-free for parents. There's a lot of space, but the kids can go only the length and breadth of the ship—a very secure environment. In addition, many ships offer a cornucopia of facilities and activities that will provide something of interest for everyone. Thus, as the parents sip Campari on their private verandah, serenely watching island peaks go by, their fourteen-year-old is having a blast playing water volleyball, while their ten-year-old goes wild in the video arcade or learns the rudiments of watercoloring.

Some cruise lines specialize in family cruising but others may provide children's programs only during certain seasons, such as summer and holiday time. Your travel agent can direct you to lines that will meet your family's needs.

❋

When you are planning the cruise, include every family member in the discussion. Make a wish list of everyone's choices and communicate the information to your travel agent.

❋

Family cruises need not be limited to the immediate family, of course. A cruise ship is a great venue for a family reunion. It's also a wonderful way to spend quality time with grandparents, cousins, close family friends, and so on.

148 Baby-sitting can be arranged at the information desk. Reserve a sitter as soon as you can.

On most ships, each passenger will be given an identification card. This card also serves as a charge card for onboard purchases. Set strict limits for the kids to follow if you are going to let them use it.

SOME FAMILY-FRIENDLY CRUISE LINES

CARNIVAL CRUISE LINE
CELEBRITY CRUISES
DISNEY CRUISE LINE
NORWEGIAN CRUISE LINE
PRINCESS CRUISES
ROYAL CARIBBEAN INTERNATIONAL

If possible, pack each child's belongings in a separate piece of children's luggage.

When packing, remember to bring a favorite stuffed animal, toy, or storybook for each child. This "security blanket" will help the child adjust to the ship.

Put together a "goodie bag" for each child containing projects to occupy them on the plane, while waiting to embark or disembark the ship, and whenever else they may get restless.

Bring along a map of the world. Each night, show your children the places you'll be passing by or visiting the next day. Enrich their understanding of where they're traveling with facts about each place and with historical and cultural information from a travel guidebook.

Even on vacation, kids tend to like routines. On the cruise, do things that are part of your everyday life: bedtime stories, nap time, regular meal hours.

Cruise ships are very different from most people's surroundings in normal life. To help your children feel comfortable, walk around the ship with them after unpacking and get familiar with the facilities.

Even eight-year-olds enjoy the thrill of spending recklessly. Give each child some money to blow on their vacation.

150 Ask one of the kids to be responsible for assembling a family scrapbook of the cruise, with photos, ticket stubs, excursion brochures, and so on.

To lend structure to the cruise, assign each child a "chore." An older sibling might baby-sit the twins late at night while the parents boogie in the disco. For their part, the twins can put away all of the kids' toys and clothes each evening before bed.

Have some brightly colored T-shirts with the name of the ship or some special symbol (for security reasons, no kids' names, please) made up for each family member. Not only will this serve as a nice memento, but it will help you find each other at a glance, onboard and off.

Most cruise lines that focus on family cruising will have cribs available. If you need one for your baby, ask your travel agent to request one for you.

If the family is in two or more cabins, buy a pair of walkie-talkies so you can communicate back and forth,

both on the ship and in a busy shopping port. It'll be
fun for the kids and will help you keep track of everyone while in port.

✳

Most ships offer a parent/child orientation with the
youth supervisors on the first day of the cruise. The
staff will provide detailed information about the
programs and help the kids choose the ones that are
right for them.

✳

Give the children some basic rules of etiquette to
follow when they are onboard the ship. (The last thing
you want is the management calling to complain about
your child's behavior.) Emphasize the importance of
the safety instructions.

✳

The drinking age onboard most cruise ships is eighteen,
because the ships will be sailing in international waters.
Teenagers should know that they will be asked for an
ID if they order alcohol.

✳

Keep a note pad in the cabin so that everyone can

152 record where they can be found throughout the day. Some cruise lines let children travel free if they stay in their parents' cabin. This will not be very appealing for some couples (or for their kids, for that matter), but for those who expect to use the cabin as a mere pit stop, it's a great deal!

When the ship is in port, older teenagers who want to venture off by themselves should be given a designated time and place to meet up with the parents. All family members should know the name of the ship in case they get lost.

The cruise program for the following day arrives in your cabin the preceding evening. At bedtime, plan the next day's schedule with the children. Find at least one activity that the entire family can participate in together. Also insist that everyone meet for dinner. It may be the only time you'll be all together during the cruise.

If your cabins are next to wild party-givers or particularly loud lovers, you might want to ask the hotel man-

ager if it is possible to be moved. Along the same lines,   153
expect courtesy from the kids—don't let them disturb
their neighbors. They shouldn't be allowed to shriek,
run in and out slamming doors, jump on the beds,
pounding on walls, and so on.

Hand-draw a simple map of the ship for younger children so it is easier for them to find their cabin. Also, let
them tape a little drawing to the outside of their cabin
door so that they can see their cabin from way down
the hall.

SINGLES

*In recent years, cruise lines have put together many pack-
ages meant to appeal particularly to single people.
Singles are a unique breed of cruisers. They are often
exceptionally adventurous, joining in many activities with
zeal and good humor. Sometimes people without part-
ners opt for a cruise geared toward singles because they
often feel excluded in our couples-oriented society; on the
cruise—or at least in various programs and activities—
they can be among the majority for a change. And, not*

154 *surprisingly, given the inherently sensual nature of cruising, many singles are looking for a little romance on the Love Boat. Or, even better, some "motion on the ocean." Olé!*

Sometimes single passengers can cruise at a lower rate during the off seasons. Ask your travel agent to look into these fares.

Beware of ships' officers who make marriage proposals or make you feel like you are the love of their life. Chances are they used the same line on another passenger on the cruise before—if not the night before! Enjoy their attentions by all means, but be realistic.

If you are accustomed to a queen- or king-size bed at home, ask the cabin steward to push the twin beds together. You'll be more comfortable, and who knows, you just may need the extra room for a romantic occasion later in the cruise.

If you are an older single man, you might qualify to cruise for free or at a considerable discount as a gentleman host. You can find out more about this program by calling the cruise lines directly.

If you don't want to be bothered by other passengers looking for a date, wear a wedding ring. This should keep most (but probably not all!) potential love interests away.

SOME SINGLES-FRIENDLY CRUISE LINES

Carnival Cruise Line

Celebrity Cruises

Club Med Cruises

Norwegian Cruise Line

Princess Cruise Line

Royal Caribbean International

Windjammer Barefoot Cruises

Opt for elegance rather than exhibitionism in your clothing. Extremely provocative swim-wear and eveningwear will likely attract more pests than princes.

If you are interested in meeting other single passengers, ask the maitre d' to seat you at a dining table with single guests.

GAYS AND LESBIANS

On some cruises, the word "cruising" takes on an entirely different meaning! The gay and lesbian cruise travel market has tripled in the past decade. Many cruise lines

156 *make a special effort to design packages that will appeal to people with nontraditional lifestyles.*

Not all travel agencies have information regarding gay and lesbian cruises. It's important to have an agent you can trust with personal information, as well as one who can provide inside tips for getting the most out of your cruise experience.

If you are interested in cruising on an all-gay cruise, call for a free brochure and list of itineraries for the year. Telephone (815) 663–3100 and ask for the RSVP cruise division.

Buy a gay/lesbian guidebook, like a *Sparticus* or *Bob Damron's* guide, before leaving on your cruise. The information in these books will provide a list of gay restaurants and other facilities in the ports of call you'll be visiting.

Ask the shore excursion staff if they can recommend different places in port that you can explore. Many times they will know of gay establishments.

Be patient, not angry or rude, to passengers who frown upon your homosexuality or bother you in any way.

When you arrive onboard the ship, ask the cruise director to help you set up a gathering. Ask her to print in the daily program: "Friends of Dorothy's get-together" or "Pink-triangle party." Most homosexuals will understand this code and come to the festivities to meet other gay people early in the cruise.

SENIORS

Many older people today have not only the time but also the financial resources to cruise the world in style—and many are doing so. Two-week, two-month, even six-month cruises to exotic ports of call around the world beckon to these discerning travelers.

Generally speaking, the longer the cruise, the older the passengers onboard the ship.

Some cruise lines sail more seniors than others (see sidebar at right for a partial list).

158 If you are looking for a relaxing cruise with no children running around the ship, ask your travel agent to suggest a couple of options.

When cruising during a holiday, you can expect several hundred children (or more!) to be onboard many of the larger cruise ships.

If you are used to going to bed or eating dinner early, start adjusting your clock to the ship's schedule a month before you go on your cruise.

Don't be afraid to talk to passengers of all ages. One of the advantages of a cruise is the opportunity to meet all sorts of people, of all ages—and for them to have the pleasure of getting to know you.

If you are dancing with one of the gentleman hosts or cruise staff, remember that they are onboard the ship for your dancing pleasure only!

A cruise is a wonderful time to renew your wedding 159 vows. It's great knowing that the person you've been married to for forty-five years would still do it all over again! Ask the captain, cruise director, or minister (if one happens to be onboard) if he will conduct the ceremony.

Beware of pushy taxi drivers in some ports of call. They may promise a certain fare and then try to take advantage of you because you're a senior citizen. Try to establish a fare in advance (in some countries, the government sets the rates). If the cabby goes over that fare, get one of the port agents to sort out the conflict.

> **SOME SENIOR-FRIENDLY CRUISE LINES**
>
> Celebrity Cruises
> Costa Cruise Lines
> Cunard Line
> Holland America Line
> Westours
> Princess Cruises
> Radisson Seven Seas Cruises
> Royal Caribbean International
> Seabourn Cruise Line
> Silversea Cruises

160 HONEYMOONERS & ROMANTICS

A kiss on the cheek while strolling on the deck or an intense gaze across the dining-room table are just a couple of the subtle ways honeymooners and romantics express their affection when sailing onboard a love boat. Cruising is the ideal vacation for those who want to enhance or rekindle their relationships.

If you have booked a cabin with two twin beds, make sure your travel agent has confirmed they can be pushed together. The last thing you want to discover is that the beds in your cabin are bolted to the floor.

A great way to begin your cruise, and a nice way to say "I love you" to the person you will be cruising with, is to order a bon voyage gift for them and have it waiting in the cabin when they arrive on the ship. Ask your travel agent to arrange the gift.

Everyone loves a lover—within reason. Spare your fellow passengers the details of your sex life. They really are not interested in watching you make out in the pool or writhe against each other on the dance floor.

If you want to impress your special someone, ask your travel agent or the shore excursion staff to inquire about a limousine service in one of the ports of call. It's a great feeling to walk down a gangway in a glamorous island port and know that the shiny limousine is all yours, waiting to escort you and your loved one around the island in utter comfort. Go all the way—arrange to have strawberries and champagne waiting inside!

If you are fairly recently married or have different last names, bring along a copy of your marriage certificate for immigration. You may need it as a form of identification.

Where better to get married than on a glorious cruise ship? Ask your travel agent to inquire with the cruise line about this option for tying the knot.

Sometimes you can get married on land and have the reception onboard while the ship is docked in port. Your guests will be thrilled, and once they leave, you

162 and your sweetheart can begin your honeymoon. Your travel agent can help with the arrangements.

If you wear your wedding dress to the ship, ask the cruise director if it can be stored in one of the costume areas. Usually there is room, and it can hang there, protected and secure, until you disembark.

Ask your cabin steward to place a red rose on your partner's pillow when preparing your cabin for the evening. Include a note written by you suggesting a bit of fun and frolic. (Don't forget to give your cabin steward a couple of dollars for helping out.)

Sit in the Jacuzzi late at night with a bottle of champagne, a bowl of strawberries, and some soft music. Ask your cabin steward to help arrange the setup. (A nice tip would be appropriate here).

If you know your loved one's favorite song, talk to the musicians beforehand and have them play the song while you are enjoying a cocktail or dance in one of

Take a walk outside late at night and steal a kiss in the moonlight. If the fireworks start exploding, go to your cabin—do not attempt to climb into one of the lifeboats!

If your cabin has a verandah or balcony, request dinner to be brought to your stateroom, and dine outside with your special someone. It is very romantic!

Buy each other something special in the onboard gift or jewelry shop to remember the wonderful time together.

PEOPLE WITH SPECIAL NEEDS

Most cruise ships are wheelchair-friendly, and so are the crew and staff who work on them. Don't hesitate for one minute if you are physically or otherwise challenged and worried about whether you will be all right on a cruise. Go for it, and have the time of your life!

164 Not all cruise ships are built to accommodate physically challenged passengers. The newer vessels, though, have terrific cabins, and it is easy to access all areas of the ship. Make sure your travel agent has specifically asked the cruise line about this, and get confirmation in writing.

Most cruise lines require physically challenged passengers to sail with an able-bodied companion. Be sure that the person you are traveling with understands his responsibilities before getting onboard the ship.

If you don't have a traveling companion, call your local hospital and ask if there are any retired nurses or aides who might be interested in going with you. You will have no problem finding one—especially, of course, if you are paying for their cruise.

Some cruise lines allow seeing-eye dogs onboard their ships, but you must get written permission in advance. Your travel agent can arrange this.

There are a limited number of wheelchair-accessible cabins available on cruise ships. Try to make your cruise travel arrangements at least a year in advance.

If you are hearing-impaired, make sure your cruise companion lets you know about any important onboard announcements.

The Society for the Advancement of Travel for the Handicapped (SATH) offers advice to people with handicaps who wish to travel. Call (212) 447–7284 for a free copy of SATH's newsletter.

Inform the hotel staff of your disability. In the event of an emergency, a special rescue party will go to your cabin and assist in taking you to your emergency boat station.

If you are physically challenged, contact the cruise director. The cruise staff will then be informed, and you can feel more comfortable about participating in entertainment and activities.

166   It is very difficult for passengers in wheelchairs to go ashore when the ship is tendering. The staff at the information desk can help arrange preboarding for you or set up a better time for you to use the tender boats.

On bus tours in ports of call, often a tour guide explains the sights over a microphone system. Remember this when booking excursions if you are hearing-impaired.

BUSINESS MEETINGS, CLUBS, AND LARGER GROUPS

I can't think of a better place to hold a business meeting than in a conference room onboard a cruise ship. Where else can you watch the head speaker stand at a podium and sway from side to side? Cruise ships are equipped with the latest technologies that allow nearly any kind of group, business committee, or club to gather together and conduct business. Next time your organization wants to hold a big meeting, suggest a cruise ship!

Large groups can receive a substantial discount on a 167 cruise. Have your travel agent contact the group department at the cruise line you wish to sail with.

Have your travel agent arrange with the cruise line to have a desk set up in the lobby area on the ship. This will give everyone traveling in your group a focal point and central area in which to meet.

Ask your travel agent to book a section of cabins in the same general area of the ship. This will give you an opportunity to keep some cabin doors open and visit from cabin to cabin. (Remember to respect the privacy and quiet times of those not involved in your party.)

Your travel agent and group department of the cruise line will be able to advise you on specific arrangements for conferences, seminars, dinners, and so on. It is no more complicated than arranging a group meeting or conference on land—but it is so much more memorable and satisfying an event!

168 Have identifying tags, T-shirts, or other mementos made up in advance and pass them out to the group members as they arrive onboard.

Contact the ship photographer to organize a group photograph.

A company called Corporate Cruises, Inc., can provide information about chartering an entire ship for your company's incentive travel and meeting space. Call (815) 663–7777 for more information.

WHEN
THE PARTY'S
OVER

You've eaten your last supper, sat on your suitcase to get it shut, and hidden your new diamond necklace in the dirty laundry to try to beat the customs man. Ready or not, it's time to go home.

Don't be too sad—as my grandma used to say, "If you don't leave, how can you come back again?" That said, it is true that you will probably feel a little blue. But you'll have happier memories of the cruise as a whole if you take a few simple steps to make the transfer home more relaxed and your readjustment to real life less jarring.

PACKING UP

It will be a lot easier to pack up at the end of the cruise than it was to pack for the cruise. Since you will probably be cleaning all of your clothes when you get home, wrinkling and organization won't be such an issue. Go ahead—throw everything in pronto so that you can enjoy every last minute of your adventure!

Don't forget to gather all of your personal items from your cabin safe or from the safe-deposit box at the purser's desk. If you forget something on the ship, contact the cruise line's corporate office. (Unfortunately, not all items are turned into the lost and found, so remember to check everywhere before you leave.)

You will be asked to place your luggage outside your cabin door the night before disembarkation; the ship's staff will take it to a central area for distribution. Make sure you have kept a change of clothing for the following day—you don't want to walk down the gangway wrapped in a shower curtain!

Roll up each piece of dirty laundry as tightly as possible and place it around any breakable items (some of these items you might prefer to carry with you).

DISEMBARKATION

Getting the passengers and luggage off the ship is typically a long and tiring process because the ship has to get clearance from the port authorities and you may have to go through immigration and customs. Instead of getting frustrated, use the time to take a last stroll around the ship, enjoy a good-bye conversation with your new friends, and to admire the views of the port where the ship has docked.

A day or so before you leave the ship, the cruise director will hold a briefing, explaining all of the procedures to follow regarding disembarkation. At least one person from each family should attend this talk, as the information will provide a smooth transition for you to leave the ship. This briefing will also give you an opportunity to ask questions. Bring a paper and pen and note the most important points.

You can realistically count on two to three hours of

174 waiting around before the actual disembarkation from the ship begins. Keep a crossword puzzle, cards, or a book handy to amuse yourself during this time.

Physically challenged passengers and any other guests needing assistance are given priority disembarkation privileges. Please don't abuse this privilege if you don't really qualify for it.

If you are on the air/sea package, you will be transferred to the airport by the cruise line representatives. The earlier your flight, the sooner you will disembark from the ship and be transferred.

On the morning of disembarkation, breakfast hours will be moved back one hour. This will be your last opportunity to eat before leaving the ship, so if you want breakfast, plan on getting up early.

Passengers are not allowed to disembark from the ship until all of the luggage has been taken off the vessel and arranged in the terminal building, usually according to a number or colored tag that you placed on your bags the night before. This procedure can take a good couple of hours. Be patient! Getting irritated won't speed it along.

✴

Porters will be available in the luggage terminal to help you transfer your bags. It is customary to tip these gentlemen $1.00 per bag.

✴

Sometimes passengers leave a ship and their cruise with a bad impression because the disembarkation process was too long or poorly organized. You can help the cruise line and yourself if you eat a leisurely breakfast, relax in your cabin or one of the public lounges, and plan an activity to amuse yourself until it is time to leave.

✴

Don't gather around the gangway area and talk to the staff in charge of helping with disembarkation. Letting them get their job done will speed the process for everyone. You'll have plenty of other opportunities to say good-bye.

176 Room service and bar service are discontinued on the morning of disembarkation.

When the captain receives clearance from the port authorities, disembarkation can begin. In some cases, not only will you have to wait for this clearance, but you will also have to pass through customs.

If there is a "lucky comment-card drawing" at the end of your cruise, make sure you enter. Sometimes cruise lines give away a discount on a future cruise. Also, be as honest as you can with your comments—the cruise lines will appreciate any advice you can give to better their product.

AFTER YOUR CRUISE

When your cruise is finished you arrive home and begin your re-entry into real life. Slowly, you will begin to get into your daily routine again—whether you want to or not. But something will feel different. You'll find that you are craving something unlike anything you've ever hungered for before. It isn't a sick feeling, but an overpowering sense of want, desire, and obsession. It is a condition called cruise-itis. (The technical name is "frequent floaters disease.") The symptoms? You can't stop talking about your cruise. You thrive on other people's cruise stories, and you even look for ways to top them. You go to your travel agent, start looking at cruise brochures again, and begin planning your next cruise.

This phase is very common, and the symptoms last only a couple of weeks. Many people go through it, so don't panic. Eventually you will get back to normal and will even enjoy your "real" life again. You'll gradually become your old self—that is, until the next cruise.

If you are on a post-land package, you may begin your tour immediately after you disembark from the ship. This means you may not see your hotel until that evening. Make sure you have had a good breakfast, are wearing comfortable clothing and shoes, and have had a stop at the rest room before the tour.

Some travel agents do a tremendous amount of work to see that you have the best cruise possible. If you

178 thoroughly enjoyed your cruise, why not send a thank-you note or perhaps give your agent a souvenir from one of the ports of call? These gestures are really appreciated.

Call the travel agency and give them feedback about your cruise, good and bad. This helps them to know whether or not to recommend that cruise ship or cruise line again.

Join the cruise line's repeat-passenger club. On your next cruise with that cruise line, you'll receive some nice gifts, an invitation to a special cocktail party, and early check-in at the pier.

If you were happy with the service you received from one particular staff member, write a letter to the cruise line corporate office and commend the cruise line for hiring such a professional person. These letters carry a tremendous amount of weight, especially when there is a possibility of promotion of a crew member.

If your cruise was a complete disaster, explain the details to your travel agent. She will contact the cruise line and attempt to get some kind of discount or refund, if the situation merits. If you feel your travel agent was the reason for the disaster, use the tips in Chapter Two to find a different cruise agent for next time.

Ask your travel agent to let you know about discounts on future cruises.

Share your good fortune. An organization called A New Voyage gives children who have successfully completed treatments for a serious illness the chance to experience a complimentary cruise. If you would like to donate to this worthwhile, nonprofit organization in order to help fund the airline flights, port charges, taxes, transfers, and other cruise-related expenses, write to A New Voyage, 117 West Saint Paul Street, Spring Valley, IL 61362-0147.

180 FINDING EMPLOYMENT ON CRUISE SHIPS

On every cruise, at least fifty people ask me about employment opportunities onboard a ship. While it is wonderful to work on a cruise ship, it is not suited for everyone. Cruise lines hire professionals, not individuals that want to get away from their boring job at home and work for a couple of weeks or months. Working onboard a ship is completely different from vacationing on one. It takes high energy, strong commitment, and long hours.

Some cruise lines receive 200 to 300 photos and résumés each month from people seeking employment. Because the demand is so great, the employees who work on cruise ships must be extremely service-oriented and have brilliant customer-service skills. They must also have some kind of training or experience in the department in which they hope to work.

If you are seriously interested in working onboard a cruise ship, contact the Cruise Staff Training Institute. You can e-mail them at cruising@ivnet.com or call

❋

Working on a cruise ship is not as glamorous as you might think. But if you like people, are willing to work long hours, and love the sea, then working on a ship may be the perfect career.

❋

Beware of scam operators promising jobs on cruise ships. No one can promise you a job except the cruise line itself. Before you order any type of book regarding employment opportunities on cruise ships, ask for the copyright date, the name and reputation of the author, and detailed information about its contents. Sometimes, even if the book has 300 pages, only 20 of those pages are related to cruise ships, and even those pages could be outdated or irrelevant.

To begin a career on a cruise ship, it is imperative that you learn the basics. Order *The Complete Cruise Ship Employment Package* for $49.05 plus $5.00 shipping. Fax orders to Cruise Concepts Inc. at (815) 663–3131.

About the Author

Jim West is one of the most sought-after speakers and foremost authorities on cruise travel today. He has sailed on more than 620 cruises, explored all seven continents (including Antarctica), and traveled to fifty-two countries. As a cruise director he has given advice to nearly one million people. Jim has worked onboard the cruise ships of Princess Cruises, Celebrity Cruises, Fantasy Cruises, and Orient Lines for a combined total of ten years.

Jim is the host of a weekly travel radio program and writes a travel column that is in the process of being syndicated. He also personally organizes and plans cruises for individuals and groups. He toured the United States for CLIA (Cruise Lines International Association) and has been called "the most effervescent, enthusiastic, and entertaining cruise director on the Seven Seas" by one of the former presidents of the American Society of Travel Agents. Jim is happy to talk to you about any of your cruise questions. Phone (815) 663–7000 or e-mail him at cruising@ivnet.com.